ELECTIONS
The People's Choice

BY
GEORGE R. LEE

COPYRIGHT © 1998 Mark Twain Media, Inc.

ISBN 10-digit: 1-58037-036-5
          13-digit: 978-1-58037-036-3

Printing No. CD-1309

Mark Twain Media, Inc., Publishers
Distributed by Carson-Dellosa Publishing LLC

Visit us at www.carsondellosa.com

Table of Contents

Introduction

It is Sunday afternoon, and the "big game" is on television. Some are bored and are reading or playing games. Some are only slightly interested and decide they are for Team "A" because their uniforms are prettier and the star is so good-looking. Others are into the game, and even though they do not understand the complex strategy, they really want Team "A" to win. They may be the hometown favorites whom observers like simply because of where they live. A few will get very excited during the game, but others will be more worried about the pizza in the oven than about which team wins.

Watching more carefully are those who truly understand the game and see the strategy at work. They look for blunders and mistakes and pronounce certain moves worth a "D" or "F." They look for the brilliant moves as well, and when the game is over, they know not only who won, but why.

For the players, the game is serious business, and the moves they and their opponents make may bring them closer to or keep them away from the victory they are trying so hard to achieve.

Political campaigns have much in common with our game, but the stakes are far greater. It has been said: "We get the kind of government we deserve." Those we elect will affect our peace, prosperity, security, and opportunities. We need to be very careful about whom we choose.

The young people who use this book may feel like they are just bystanders during a political campaign, but while they cannot vote, they can begin to understand what is going on and find ways to become involved.

Citizen involvement is the key to a successful democracy, and the sooner young people feel they are part of the process, the more likely they are to watch candidates carefully and keep them in line.

Political Terms

ABSENTEE VOTING - Allows a person to vote by mail rather than at the polls.

ACTIVIST - Person very active in politics who does not hold public office.

AUSTRALIAN BALLOT - Secret ballot.

AVAILABILITY - Likely candidate for a high office.

BALANCING THE TICKET - Choosing a running mate to attract a different segment of
  voters than the candidate could draw on his or her own.

BALLOT - List of candidates to be selected by voters in the election. "Long ballot" has a
  long list to be voted upon; "short ballot" lists only a small number.

BELLWEATHER PRECINCTS - Those precincts that are accurate predictors of how the
  election will go.

CAMPAIGN - Process for electing a candidate.

CAMPAIGN FINANCE - The money donated to support the campaign. Money given to a
  candidate that is limited in amount is called "hard money;" money given to a PAC is
  "soft money" and may be given in unlimited amounts.

CAUCUS - Closed meeting of party leaders or members.

CANDIDATE - A person running for office.

CHARISMA - Special personal qualities that attract wide support.

COATTAILS - Tendency of some voters to cast votes for candidates of the ticket leader's
  party.

CONSERVATIVE - A person who wants limited government involvement in the economy.

CONSTITUENT - A resident of a legislator's district.

DARK HORSE - A candidate rarely mentioned for higher office before he or she is chosen
  when better-known candidates block each other out.

DEMOCRACY - Government by the people. "Pure" democracy is one where the citizens
  make the decisions. "Representative" democracy is one where citizens choose those
  who will make the decisions.

ELECTION - Process of choosing officials by casting votes.

ELECTORAL COLLEGE - Those who have the formal duty of choosing the U. S. president.

FAVORITE SON - Candidate chosen by a state or local party to nominate at a political
  convention.

FILING - Required act of putting one's name on the ballot.

GENERAL ELECTION - A statewide or national election to choose officeholders.

GERRYMANDER - The drawing of district lines to benefit a political party.

INCUMBENT - The person presently holding an office.

INDEPENDENT - A person with no loyalty to either political party.

INITIATIVE - Process by which citizens pass around petitions on a public issue; when it has
  met legal requirements and receives a majority in an election, it becomes law.

LIBERAL - A person wanting government to be an important part of the economy.

LOCAL OFFICE - One with authority in a city or county.

MEDIA - The communication system, including television, newspapers, and radio.

NATIONAL CHAIRMAN - Controls the staff of a political party.

NATIONAL COMMITTEE - Chosen party officials who oversee work of national party between conventions.

NOMINEE - The candidate chosen by the party to run in the general election.

NONPARTISAN ELECTION - The party of the candidates is not shown on the ballot.

ONE-PARTY STATE - A state that almost always supports the same party, and the weaker party is poorly organized to campaign.

PACK - The group of reporters following a candidate around the country.

PARTISAN ELECTION - The party affiliation of candidates is shown on the ballot.

PIVOTAL STATE - One that is very important to winning the election.

POLITICAL ACTION COMMITTEE (P.A.C.) - A group pushing a special interest; it contributes to candidates supporting its view.

PLATFORM - The official party position on public issues. The position on each public issue is called a "plank."

POLITICAL PARTY - Loosely organized group dedicated to choosing public officials.
> "Two-party system" - the dominance of Democrats and Republicans.
> "Third party" - a protest movement running candidates capable of winning the election.
> "Minor party" - has a cause it wants to present, but has no chance of winning.

POLITICIAN - A person elected to public office or active in politics.

POLITICS - The science of public affairs, including the election system and the decision-making processes of government.

PRESS CONFERENCE - An opportunity for the candidate or press secretary to distribute information to reporters.

PRESSURE GROUP - Organized interest group.

PRIMARY - System of choosing party candidates to run in a general election.

PUBLIC OPINION POLL - Asks citizens how they feel about candidates or issues. The person doing this work is the "pollster."

RECALL - A vote on whether to remove a public official before his or her term is up.

REFERENDUM - A citizen vote to approve a decision made by a legislative body.

SPIN DOCTOR - An advisor who tries to put the best possible interpretation on the candidate's campaign.

SPLIT VOTE - Voting for candidates from more than one party.

STRAIGHT TICKET - Voting for every candidate on one party's ticket.

TYRANNY - Where a ruler or small group makes all political decisions.

VOTING QUALIFICATIONS - Requirements that must be met to be a voter.

The Anytown School Student Council Election

Anytown School has a wide cross section of the community. In one class, there are five students from Ritzy Hill, with its big mansions and swimming pools. Seven students are from "the Valley," Anytown's slum. As for the other students, five are from blue-collar families; their mothers and fathers work for low wages in the factory. The other 13 students are from white-collar families of employees and small store owners. Fifteen class members are girls, and 15 are boys.

A student council election is to be held at Anytown School, and each classroom will choose a representative. Four people from the above-mentioned class would really like to be chosen: Fred, Bill, Sally, and Laura. Fred can only find three class members who like him better than Bill, so he drops out. Sally is told by her friends that if she makes it possible for a boy to win by splitting the female vote, they will never speak to her again. She drops out. Those remaining in the contest are Bill and Laura. Each is determined to win.

Bill goes around reminding his friends of favors he has done for them. Laura begins to tell classmates about what she will do once she has been elected. Their friends go around trying to persuade others to vote for their candidate. Bill's friends soon discover there is no point in trying to persuade Laura's closest friends, and Laura soon finds out the same thing about Bill's friends. Whom do they concentrate on then? They try to convince those class members who are not close to either Bill or Laura.

Each side begins thinking about a slogan. Bill's friends decide on "Bill is one of us," and Laura's slogan is "Laura makes things happen." Supporters of each candidate make signs, some of which tell students why they should vote for their candidate, and others that tell why students should not vote for the opponent.

The teacher suggests that each candidate give a five-minute speech as part of his or her campaign. Bill stands in front and reminds everyone of how he has helped them in the past; if elected, he promises to defeat their arch rival Bigandtall School in basketball this year. Laura tells them some of the things she would like to accomplish on the student council. If elected, she promises to cut the school day by 15 minutes.

Tempers flare at times between supporters of each candidate. Bill's friends whisper that Laura is a Ritzy Hill snob, and Laura's friends say that he's a dumb Valley kid. When Laura's father offers to supply the pizza for a class party, her friends claim that it was just a birthday party for his daughter. Bill's friends say that anyone voting for Laura is doing it just because she is rich, but she is not like them.

The same ingredients are at work in this classroom that are part of the political system. A job is to be filled, and candidates step forward who want the job. Bill and Laura are candidates who want to sit on the student council. Some in the class are what we call "activists," eager supporters of a candidate. The activists are the ones making signs and

4

trying to convince the others that they have the candidate who should win. There are also those who do not care who wins.

On the day of the election, the teacher gives each student a piece of paper and tells them to vote for the candidate of their choice. The votes are counted, and the name of the winner is put on the board for the class, the school, and the world to see.

Candidates, campaigning, issues, and making speeches are all part of the process by which either Laura or Bill will get elected to the student council, and perhaps later be elected as a school board member, alderman, mayor, sheriff, county clerk, state legislator, senator, governor, or president.

Your family may be one that gets excited over politics, and they may keep up with those who hold public office (politicians). They are devoted to their political party. They have definite positions on issues and support Candidate "A" because he or she is "right" on issues, or oppose Candidate "B" because he or she is "wrong" on the issues. They may be enthusiastic about a political party and want all of its candidates to win.

Your family may be one that gets interested in only the presidential, senate, or governor's race. Once the race is over, they have little interest in politics until the next election.

Or you may have a family that finds politics boring. They think that all politicians are in it for personal gain or are only concerned with helping those who have contributed to their campaign. They think that campaigns are all dirty, and no candidate is worth supporting. The sooner the campaign is over, the happier they will be.

In a few years, you will be 18 years old, and you will be eligible to vote for candidates seeking public office. A few years later, you may decide that you are interested in running yourself. It will no longer be choosing who will be a representative on the student council, but those who hold elected office in your community, county, state, and nation. The people chosen will have the power to raise or lower taxes and decide whether to spend money on education, the elderly, road improvements, the environment, or fighting crime.

You will have to decide whether to be a candidate yourself or maybe support someone who is running for office. If you do this, you will be like the person playing the game on the court or one of the enthusiastic cheerleaders and fans in the stands.

However, you could be the person who says: "I don't understand this politics stuff. It doesn't matter much to me who gets elected. Let someone else do the choosing." If you do, you will be like the person sitting outside the gym who feels neither the joy of victory nor the disappointment of defeat. You will have missed out on the entire process.

Name _____ Date _____

Challenges

1. "Divide and conquer" means to split the opponent's vote so your candidate can get the majority. Why were some boys encouraging Sally to stay in the race?

_____

_____

2. "Dropping out" is also part of politics. Why did Fred decide not to run?

_____

_____

3. Why did both sides work the undecideds rather than try to change the minds of those loyal to the other candidate?

_____

_____

4. Split loyalties are part of politics. Why would a boy from Ritzy Hills feel divided about how to vote?

_____

_____

5. Why might a girl from the Valley have wanted to support Bill?

_____

6. "Pie in the sky" promises are those that candidates may make, but they have no way of achieving them. What "pie in the sky" promise did Bill make?

_____

7. What "pie in the sky" promise did Laura make?

_____

8. Activists are the enthusiastic supporters who help candidates get elected but do not run themselves. How were the activists helping these candidates?

_____

_____

9. The class used paper ballots. Why might the election results have been changed if they had raised hands instead?

_____

_____

10. Why was it good for the students to take part in this election?

_____

_____

Name _____ Date _____

Questions to Consider

1. Why do some people like politics, and why do some hate it?

_____

_____

_____

_____

_____

_____

2. Which slogan would appeal to the most students in the class? Why?

_____

_____

_____

_____

_____

3. Laura's father offered to buy pizza for the class on his daughter's birthday. He was not thinking about the election when he did it. How do you think the undecided students would view it?

_____

_____

_____

_____

_____

Activity

Bill and Laura both used pressure to win. Which one does your class think deserved to win? Which one would probably make the better student council representative?

Elections: The Basic Element of Democracy

Democracy literally means "government by the people." Abraham Lincoln defined it as "government of the people, by the people, for the people." In *pure democracy*, the citizens themselves decide what they want to do.

In ancient Greece, large meetings were held, the citizens listened to the arguments on both sides, and then they voted. The side with the most votes won. In small New England towns, pure democracy is still practiced at town meetings. Town meeting decisions tell officials what they must do.

Representative democracy is the system used when the population is too large for a meeting. The citizens choose someone to represent their interests and send that person to the city council, state legislature, or to Washington as their representative or senator. We allow someone else to make decisions for us. If we don't like the decisions they make, we vote them out of office in the next election.

This is different from *tyranny,* where the ruler or a small group makes all major decisions, and no one has the power to remove him or her from office. Adolf Hitler is a good example of a tyrant. In Nazi Germany (1933–1945), he spoke, and the people listened. He ordered, and they obeyed. In the early days, the legislature (Reichstag) voted approval of his policies, but in time, he did away with even that and ruled alone. A tyrant tells the newspapers and media what to say. All officials, including police and judges, must carry out the tyrant's wishes.

Some tyrannies pretend to be democratic, but no one is fooled. In Communist Russia, the people were required to vote, but there was only one candidate for each office. China in the 1990s kept iron control over those who would speak out against the government but began allowing individuals the freedom to start their own businesses. In some countries, the party in control allows other political parties to exist but will not give them use of the newspapers or radio to persuade people to vote for them. Some countries have had the same political party in power for so many years that no other potential leaders know how to run a country. Some countries allow the citizens to vote, but they throw away ballots cast for their opponents, or they have friendly voters casting several ballots. In some elections, there have been more votes cast than there were voters.

Democracy involves more than just the right to vote. It involves the right to express opinions openly and without fear, an individual's right to reach his or her own limits, and protection for the rights of minorities, including those who oppose the leaders. In democratic countries, leaders know they serve at the will of the people, and if they lose an election, they step down.

ELECTIONS are critical to rule by the people. The right to vote grew gradually in the United States. In colonial America, limits were set on who was eligible to vote. Some colonies had religious tests, and if you did not belong to the right church, you could not vote. Many had property qualifications, and if you did not own enough property, you could not vote. These requirements were higher for those who wanted to be candidates for public office. Women and blacks were not allowed to vote. Residence requirements said you had to live in the colony for a year before you could vote. The right to vote was made more difficult if you lived far away from the county seat where the voting took place. Later, a literacy test was imposed in some states to keep African-Americans and ignorant whites from voting. All of these methods limited power to those who had the power and wanted to keep it.

In the early days, there was no secrecy when voting. The voter stepped in front of the table where the clerk sat and told him which candidate he was voting for, while everyone around listened. Then political parties developed ballots, but each ballot was a different color, so everyone watched which ballot the voter picked. That method was used until the *Australian ballot* was finally developed. Since 1888, all states have used this ballot, which lists all of the candidates on one ballot, so no one knows how you voted.

In time, different groups who had been denied the right to vote received that right from the states and, eventually, by amendments to the Constitution. The Fifteenth Amendment was ratified in 1870, and it said that no one could be denied to vote on the basis of race or color. The Nineteenth Amendment was ratified in 1920. It said that no one could be denied the right to vote on the basis of gender. The poll tax (a tax that was paid before a person could vote) was removed by the Twenty-fourth Amendment in 1964. The Twenty-sixth Amendment in 1971 said that no one over 18 years old could be denied the right to vote on the basis of age. The first Voting Rights Act was passed in 1965 and was expanded later. Among the changes it made were limiting residence requirements in presidential elections to only 30 days and protecting the right of minorities to vote where experience indicated they had been denied their rights in the past.

There are still some restrictions on voting. Those who have not reached 18 years of age do not get to vote; those legally insane or in prison cannot vote. Those who have failed to register are not allowed to vote.

In addition to voting for candidates for public office, we also vote on other issues. Some states allow initiative, referendum, and recall. INITIATIVE is when the voters decide they want something that the legislature does not want to do. If they can get enough signatures on petitions, the voters are allowed to vote for or against the petition. If the majority vote yes, it becomes law. A REFERENDUM is a vote on an issue; a common one is a school bond issue, where voters decide whether to raise taxes to build a new school. RECALL is when voters decide they do not want to wait until an officeholder's term is up to remove him from office. In a recall election, whether the person deserves to remain in office is the only question. He is not running against an opponent, but against his record. If the majority wants him out, he loses his job.

Name _____   Date _____

Challenges

1. What is pure democracy?

_____

_____

2. Why does the United States use representative democracy instead?

_____

_____

3. What happens to an elected official who makes the public angry?

_____

_____

4. What information do the people have in a tyranny?

_____

_____

5. What was the property qualification for voting?

_____

_____

6. Why did some states have a literacy test?

_____

_____

7. How did the Australian ballot protect the voter?

_____

_____

8. Who got to vote first, African-American men or white women?

_____

_____

9. If the legislature does not want to cut its size, what tool is available to the citizens in some states that does it directly?

_____

_____

10. If the citizens want to "fire the bum" before an official's term is up, what tool may they use in some states?

_____

_____

Name _____ Date _____

Points to Consider

1. Is it possible to have democracy where there is no free speech or free press?

_____

_____

_____

_____

_____

_____

2. Why is protection of minority rights an important part of democracy?

_____

_____

_____

_____

_____

_____

3. Why do some people think that the referendum is so important?

_____

_____

_____

_____

_____

Activity

Look at recent election results in your county or state, and then figure the percentage of eligible citizens who voted. Why does the class think more did not vote?

Comparing Election Systems

You may read in the newspaper that the British government is holding a general election or that the French government has fallen. Either of these events could take place at any time in any year. On the other hand, U. S. elections for national office and many state offices take place in even-numbered years. They are as regular as the clock. The War of 1812 did not stop off-year elections from being held in 1814. In 1864, the United States was fighting the Civil War, but the presidential election took place on schedule. During World War I, the Republicans took control of Congress away from the Democrats in the 1918 off-year election. And in 1944, during World War II, Republicans campaigned hard against the Democratic president, Franklin D. Roosevelt. No American leader, no matter how badly he wanted to keep his job, has ever suggested calling off an election. If he did, he would surely be impeached. Each nation may use different means to achieve the democratic form of government that suits it best.

THE BRITISH SYSTEM is called "constitutional monarchy." The position of king or queen is hereditary (they inherit the job), but the real power is in the hands of *Parliament.* There are two houses of Parliament: the *House of Commons* and the *House of Lords*, with Commons being the most important. Members of the Commons are elected; most are chosen in the "general election," where all member seats are up for election. A few come in "by elections" to replace a member who has died or resigned. General elections are quick, usually over in a few weeks.

The *prime minister* ("P.M.") is chosen by the ruler from the party with the most seats in Parliament. The prime minister forms a *Government,* the ministers who run the government departments. A special group of these are the inner circle advisors to the P.M., known as the *Cabinet.* The Government draws up most bills that are presented to the Commons. If the members vote against an important bill, it becomes a "vote of no confidence." The P.M. and Cabinet resign, and the P.M. may advise the queen to "dissolve" Parliament. When that happens, a general election follows.

The second-largest party is called "Her [or His] Majesty's Loyal Opposition," and its leader is the "leader of the Opposition." The Loyal Opposition's job is to offer alternative policies to those of the Government. The leader appoints the "Shadow Cabinet," which points out any failures of the Government. Unlike the United States, the British have three large parties: the Conservatives, Labour, and Liberal parties. Their system is also different because even though they have local governments called "councils," local officials receive much of their money from the central government.

FRANCE has a government led by a president who appoints the *premier* (or prime minister) and the *Council of Ministers* (cabinet). The premier, not the president, runs the government. Members of the National Assembly are called *deputies.* The French have many political parties, and the premier often has to persuade other parties to help him form the cabinet. When a disagreement occurs between members of the Council, the president may dissolve the Assembly and call new elections.

The governments of Great Britain and France are called *unitary,* with power in the hands of the central government. Local officials have no power of their own; they can only do what the central authorities allow. Their systems are much different from that in the United States.

The UNITED STATES has a *federal* system, with powers divided between the federal (national) government and the states. The states cannot be destroyed by the federal government, and the federal government cannot be destroyed by the states. Each has powers under the Constitution.

The U. S. Constitution created a national government with the executive branch headed by the *president,* who is picked by the Electoral College to serve a four-year term. The Congress is composed of the *Senate* (sometimes called the "upper house") and the *House of Representatives* (lower house). Senators are chosen for six-year terms by voters of the states they represent, and House members are elected for two-year terms by voters in their districts. The Constitution limits the president to two four-year terms (Twenty-second Amendment), but members of Congress are not limited in how many times they can be re-elected.

The *governor* is the leader of state government, and he is elected by the qualified voters of the state. All state legislatures have two houses except Nebraska, which has one. The size of the legislatures have nothing to do with the population. The smallest is Alaska's, and the largest is New Hampshire's. California's lower house is one-fifth the size of New Hampshire's. In addition, there are many local officials including city council aldermen, members of park and ambulance boards, school boards, coroners, county clerks, and so on. Many of these are elected in *nonpartisan* elections; in those, there are no party labels. Others are chosen in *partisan* elections, with the party name clearly labeled above its candidates.

The states have much to do with national politics. They set the boundaries for Congressional districts. They set rules for primaries. A strong state political party is a big help to its presidential candidate. State government is the source of many who move on to federal positions in Congress, the Cabinet, and the presidency.

Our federal system creates 51 political parties, the national organization, and state organizations. Unlike England and France, the national party has no control over the state party, and state parties have no control over who runs in its primaries on their label.

Three national systems have been studied, each with a different way of accomplishing the same goal: providing government for their people. In the same way, American states, counties, and cities differ from each other in how to choose leaders to achieve their goals. That is the democratic way.

Name _____ Date _____

Challenges

1. What were two examples of times when wars did not stop American presidential elections from being held?

_____

_____

2. Which is the most important house of Parliament? What is the election called in which members of Parliament are chosen?

_____

_____

3. Who picks the P.M.? Why is that person chosen?

_____

_____

4. What name is given to the second-largest British party?

_____

5. What is the job of the "Shadow Cabinet"?

_____

_____

6. Which has a job most different from the others: U. S. president, British prime minister, or French premier?

_____

_____

7. How many years do U. S. senators and representatives each serve?

_____

_____

8. What is the difference between a partisan and nonpartisan election?

_____

_____

9. Who sets the boundaries for Congressional districts?

_____

_____

10. Do national parties in the United States control state parties?

_____

_____

Name _____ Date _____

Points to Consider

1. Do you think the minority party in the United States thinks of itself as the "Shadow government"? Can you think of any examples that support your view?

_____

_____

_____

_____

_____

_____

2. Is it better to have a system that runs by the calendar or one like the British system when it follows a vote of no confidence?

_____

_____

_____

_____

_____

_____

3. In the British and French systems, the leader in the government is from the party that won the election. In 1996, President Clinton (Democrat) won the presidency, but the Republicans carried both houses of Congress. Which do you think is the better system?

_____

_____

_____

_____

_____

_____

Activity

Collect information from newspapers, magazines, and the Internet on foreign countries and their political systems. Display the information in a chart or poster to be put on the bulletin board.

American Political Parties

Imagine an opening session of the House of Representatives: 435 men and women in the room. Someone stands on a desk and says: "Who wants to be Speaker of the House?" All the hands go up. In the Senate, the presiding officer, the Vice President, tries to conduct business, but there is no organization, and confusion is everywhere. Government under these circumstances would be difficult, if not impossible. If political parties served no other purpose, it would be to organize legislative bodies.

Over the years, many have been critical of political parties. George Washington warned against forming them, saying that party spirit "agitates the community with ill-founded jealousies and false alarms." However, Thomas Jefferson said: "If I could not go to heaven without a party, I would not go there at all." Will Rogers, the humorist, said: "The more you read and observe about this Politics thing, you've got to admit that each party is worse than the other. The one that's out always looks the best."

Criticisms of political parties are common in the press, and many assume the nation would be better off without them. Despite all that has been said against them, political parties are important to the nation. At the Constitutional Convention in 1787, James Madison said: "No free country has ever been without parties, which are a natural offspring of freedom." What are these creatures, so disliked by some, so essential to others?

POLITICAL PARTIES DEFINED. A political party is a group of individuals held together by the desire to put its members in office to control the processes of government. In many countries, political parties are well-organized, and all candidates must agree to the national party positions. Some leaders of U. S. parties have at times considered making a statement that would bind all party candidates, but this has not happened.

Political parties should not be confused with special interests. They are groups of people who desire to influence government by trying to get friendly candidates elected, but they have a short list of things they want to do. The AARP wants benefits for the older citizens, the NRA wants to prevent government restrictions on gun owners, the AFL-CIO wants to help organized labor, and so on. However, they have no interest in making the wide range of domestic and foreign policies a party does.

WHY DO WE HAVE POLITICAL PARTIES? They do a number of things.

1. They help organize government. With political parties, you do not have the 435 House members screaming "Choose me." Instead, an orderly process occurs as Democrats and Republicans meet to choose party leaders and decide who will sit on committees.

2. They create interest in government. Theodore Roosevelt said that the White House was a "bully pulpit." In other words, the political party that controls the presidency can influence the ways people view issues. In the same way, those who oppose the president's policies have plenty of opportunities to criticize the way government is working and offer ideas about how improvements can be made.

Those who want to make changes in education, health care, environmental policy, farm programs, and so forth, know that the best way to get the things they want is through influencing parties to support their views.

3. They recruit candidates and campaign workers. When Officeholder "A" decides to run again on the "X" ticket, "Y" party tries to find someone to run against him or her. They look for intelligent, appealing candidates and persuade them to compete against "A." "B" agrees to run, and "B" then finds people who will back her or his campaign with money, time, and effort.

A change that has occurred in recent years is that "B" is much more likely to be a woman or from a minority group. This encourages interest among citizens who may not have been enthused before.

4. They raise money for political campaigns. "B" was not a rich person and did not know many rich people. Campaigning would be impossible without the party helping "B" raise money. The help may be indirect, giving "B" and her staff training and helping with campaign research. It may also be a direct contribution to the campaign by sending money or well-known speakers to encourage support. The better "B" seems to be doing in the campaign against "A," the more likely "B" is to get support from the party.

5. It gives the individual more reasons to get involved in the political process. They make friends at party rallies and find others who share their enthusiasm for talking about the issues. They feel like part of a team working toward election victory. They encourage others to join their cause and feel their enthusiasm for the party and its candidates. They urge others to get out and vote. When the election results come in, they feel the joy of victory or the agony of defeat.

THE ORGANIZATION OF U. S. POLITICAL PARTIES. Both of the major parties have national, state, and local organizations. The national party is governed by policies of the *national convention.* It meets once every four years and chooses the presidential and vice-presidential candidates, writes the party platform, makes rules, elects the national committee, and chooses the national chairman. The national chairman is selected from a list of one; he or she is picked by the party's nominee for president.

The conventions are much too large to run the party between their meetings. They leave the job of running the staff at national headquarters to the national chairman. Any decisions that need to be made between national conven-

tions are made by the *national committees.* The Democrat's national committee has over 400 members; the Republican committee is less than half that size. The staffs of both parties have increased substantially since the 1970s, and they focus on public relations, computerized mailing lists, research, and fund-raising between elections. The goal of each national party is to gain wide public support for the party and its candidates.

Name _____ Date _____

Challenges

1. Who felt political parties divided the people and caused unnecessary concerns?

_____

2. Who felt they were to be expected in a free nation?

_____

3. What is an important difference between political parties and special interest groups?

_____

_____

_____

4. How did the fact that "B" decided to run encourage others to get involved?

_____

_____

5. Why is the political party a good chance to get acquainted and involved?

_____

_____

6. Who sets policies for the national parties?

_____

_____

7. What is the main job of the national convention?

_____

_____

8. Who runs the day-to-day operations at national headquarters?

_____

_____

9. In 1972, the Democratic vice-presidential nominee resigned from the ticket after the convention. Who chose his successor?

_____

10. What are normal activities at party national headquarters?

_____

_____

_____

_____

Name _____ Date _____

Points to Consider

1. Why do you think Washington and Jefferson took the views they did?

_____

_____

_____

_____

_____

2. Why do special interest groups have close contact with political parties, and why do parties try to appeal to special interests?

_____

_____

_____

_____

_____

3. Why do individuals get involved in politics when they have no interest in running for an office?

_____

_____

_____

_____

_____

Activity

Pick an issue and write a plank for the platform on that subject. For example, "Should smoking be allowed in public places?" Try to make the plank one that will be popular with as many voters as possible. Then make a list of all the groups that would support it and all that would oppose it. See if you can rewrite it in such a way that those who might oppose it would accept it.

The U. S. Two-Party System

Many may find it hard to believe, but Americans have not always chosen between Democrats and Republicans. During Washington's administration, the two parties that developed were Alexander Hamilton's Federalists and Thomas Jefferson's Republicans. The Federalists faded after the War of 1812, and for a time, everyone was a Republican. In the 1824 election, the party split wide open; those who supported John Quincy Adams were National Republicans, and Andrew Jackson's supporters were Democratic-Republicans. Jackson won, and his party was soon called simply Democrats. Those who disliked Jackson formed the Whig party in the 1830s. Both Democrats and Whigs struggled over the slavery issue, and in 1854, unhappy Democrats joined with Whigs in forming the Republican party. Since then, these two parties have dominated American politics.

WHY DO WE HAVE TWO MAJOR PARTIES when the British have three major parties and the French have many? A number of reasons are given.

1. Tradition. We have had two major parties almost from the beginning, and it is the system we accept. No one alive can remember the time when there were any major parties except Democrats and Republicans to compete in more than one or two elections. It is unlikely that any other party will soon rise to challenge that record.

2. It is practical. If we don't like President "A," the best way to defeat his re-election is to unite behind Candidate "B." If those who dislike President "A" divided their support behind "B," "C," and "D," "A" would probably win. The party out of power is likely to draw support from all who are unhappy with the person in office.

3. They have the loyalty of party officeholders, financial resources, and media contacts that give them advantages over competitors.

4. The rules favor them. They are automatically placed on election ballots, while other parties have to prove they have enough support. Their candidates, assuming they accept restrictions under federal election law, are given federal election funds. Other candidates have to prove they have enough popular support to get the funds.

5. The United States has always had winner-take-all elections. This means that only one candidate will be chosen as Senator, no matter how many run. In some European countries, if Party "G" gets only five percent of the votes, it will be entitled to five percent of the seats in the legislature. This does not happen in American elections.

In the contests between Democrats and Republicans, the rivalry is not without some good humor. In 1985, one Republican said that the Democrats "could not win unless things got worse, and things would not get worse unless the Democrats were elected." In 1976, a Democrat said that "for a working man or woman to vote Republican this year is like a chicken voting for Colonel Sanders." For all the bickering and struggle that goes on between the two parties, the truth is that many friendships develop between the active workers in the two parties. They enjoy the debate and contest. When the election is over, the loser shakes hands with the winner, and the losing party prepares to win the next time.

The two parties are evenly matched. In presidential elections from the end of World War II through 1996, the Democrats won in 1948, 1960, 1964, 1976, 1992, and 1996. The Republicans won in 1952, 1956, 1968, 1972, 1980, 1984, and 1988. Some elections have been very one-sided, but the losing party came back strong in the following election. Many times, the president has been of one party, but the opposing party has had a majority in Congress. Both the president and the "loyal opposition" in Congress know they must work together and make compromises both sides can live with.

The two parties have much in common, and on many subjects, they think alike. Both are strongly patriotic and believe in the free enterprise system. Both represent a wide variety of people and interests. Neither wants to destroy the rights of citizens or create a different legal system. They know that any attempt to move away from these principles would ruin any chance of winning the election.

There are some differences between the two. While there are many exceptions to the characteristics we will discuss, these are the often-mentioned stereotypes (a view held by a number of people) of the parties.

REPUBLICANS. The Republican stereotype is a white person of middle to upper class, in favor of big business, defense spending, lower taxes, and suspicious of government. As President Ronald Reagan put it: "I believe that government is the problem, not the answer." They often campaign on moral issues, concern for the future of the family, and religion. In urban areas, Republicans are far more likely to live in the suburbs than in the city.

DEMOCRATS. The Democratic stereotype is a person of lower income, working class, concerned with issues like the environment, the rights of unions, and raising taxes and cutting defense spending to provide more aid for education and social services. The Democrat often feels that government can solve many of the problems faced by those who are poor or less educated. The Democrat is far more likely to be a minority member and live in the city.

Within each party, there are often strong disagreements. In 1964, the very conservative Senator, Barry Goldwater, won the Republican nomination for president despite the protests of more liberal party members. The liberals refused to support Goldwater, and he lost the election by 16 million votes. The Democrats divided in 1972 over the choice of the very liberal George McGovern, and he lost by 19 million votes. In the next election, the party that had lost so badly before won this time, proving that the two-party system shows an amazing ability to survive.

Name _____ Date _____

Challenges

1. What were the first two U. S. political parties?

_____

_____

2. Who was the first president to officially be a Democrat?

_____

_____

3. What issue led to the formation of the Republican party?

_____

_____

On the lines below, put the number of the reason we have two parties.

4. Splitting the opposition helps you win. _____

5. It helps to have friends in high places. _____

6. It helps if the person recognizes your name. _____

7. If presidential elections from 1948 to 1996 were a game, which party would be ahead and by what score (1 point for each victory)?

_____

_____

8. Which part of the urban area is more likely to be a Democrat's home?

_____

_____

9. Which party seems to favor defense spending and business?

_____

_____

10. Who lost by the larger margin: Goldwater or McGovern?

_____

_____

Name _____ Date _____

Points to Consider

1. Some critics say that the reason we only have two major parties is because they made all the rules. Do you think that a change in rules would make it possible for a third party to challenge them?

_____

_____

_____

_____

_____

2. Are the two parties more alike than they are different?

_____

_____

_____

_____

_____

3. How can each party claim that it is the party that best represents the American people?

_____

_____

_____

_____

_____

Activity

Look up the two parties on the Internet. See what information is available that would help you understand American politics. Their addresses are:

DEMOCRAT - http://www.democrats.org   REPUBLICAN - http://www.gop.com

23

Third Parties:
The Political Wild Cards

In 1968, strange things happened in American politics. President Lyndon Johnson, elected by a huge majority in 1964, was very unpopular, and he chose not to try for another term. After a popular Democratic candidate, Robert Kennedy, was killed, Vice President Humphrey finally won the Democratic nomination. With the Democrats split on social issues and the war in Vietnam, it appeared that the Republican nominee, Richard Nixon, would easily win the election. Then, out of nowhere, came Governor George Wallace, who was against those "liberals, intellectuals, and long-hairs" who had run the nation too long. Creating the American Independent party, he appealed to many who felt the nation was heading in the wrong direction. If elected, he would shoot rioters, win the war, put welfare cheats in jail, and take power from the federal government and give it back to the states.

The Nixon campaign was in trouble, not because of what Humphrey was doing, but because Wallace was appealing to many of those who Nixon thought would vote for him. Wallace had no chance of winning, but it was possible that he would keep Nixon or Humphrey from winning. The Constitution says that if no one has the majority in the electoral vote, the House chooses the president. In a year when anything was possible, this could provide the strangest drama of all.

Wallace was playing the role of a third-party candidate: to raise issues others were ignoring and attack the two-party system. In the end, he failed to win the presidency or throw the election into the House, but he got 13 percent of popular votes, received 46 electoral votes, and kept Nixon from sweeping the South.

The goal of the third party is to appeal to enough voters who are unhappy with the other parties so they may have an influence on the election and the laws that are passed. They are rarely successful in becoming a real challenge, but exceptions exist. One occurred in the 1890s when the Populist party was formed. Populists were mostly Southern and Western farmers and mine owners who were angry with both parties for their pro-business attitudes. Among the changes they demanded were a graduated income tax, the direct election of senators, initiative and recall. In 1892, their candidate for president received over one million popular votes and 22 electoral votes. Both parties called the Populists radicals and warned of national disaster if they ever won. Populist popularity grew when hard times hit the nation in 1893. In 1896, William Jennings Bryan, a Democrat with broad appeal among Populists, was nominated. The Populists chose him as their candidate as well, and the Populists ceased to exist. However, the things they wanted eventually became federal and state laws.

In 1912, former Republican president Theodore Roosevelt was so angered by the policies of President Taft that he challenged Taft in the Republican convention. Claiming the convention was rigged against him (which it was), Roosevelt became the Progressive party (often called the Bull Moose party) candidate, and he received 600,000 more popular and 80 more electoral votes than Taft in the election. But because of the Republican split, a Democrat, Woodrow Wilson, won.

The most recent example of a third party was that formed very quickly in 1992 by billionaire H. Ross Perot. Claiming that both parties were corrupt and saying he could end the gridlock between the president and Congress in Washington, over two million people offered to help in the effort to get his name on the ballot in all 50 states. His Independent party failed to win any electoral votes but won 19 percent of popular votes.

These examples point out several qualities of a third party. (1) The people who form them are angry. (2) They find a dynamic leader who expresses their frustration. (3) They develop a platform that appeals to their supporters. (4) They scare one or both of the major parties, who charge that these "radicals" are a menace to the nation. (5) They lose the election. (6) Some of their ideas are later accepted and become law.

WHY THEY DON'T WIN. The third party faces several problems.

1. They lack money. Unlike the established parties, they do not have money held back for the campaign, and it is difficult for them to borrow.

2. They lack organization. The major parties are organized at the local, state, and national levels. They have public officials (mayors, sheriffs, county clerks, state, and national office holders) who have an interest in seeing that their party wins. The third party does not have this built-in support to rely on.

3. Many voters may agree with them on the issues but feel it is wasting their vote to cast it for someone who has no chance of winning. It is hard for a third party to persuade them to believe the party really has a chance.

4. They face an enormous task in getting on the ballot. States have all kinds of requirements that must be met for a candidate to be placed on the ballot. Unless everything is done properly and by the deadline, the name is left off the ballot, and the candidate has no chance to win there.

MINOR PARTIES are similar to third parties in the sense that they have a definite opinion and are often made up of angry people, but they have little or no impact on national politics. There are a variety of types of minor parties.

Left-wing parties are dedicated to major changes or the destruction of the free enterprise system. These include Socialist and Communist parties.

One-issue parties have a particular issue that drives them. Examples include the Prohibition party and the Vegetarian party.

One-state parties may affect who wins elections by supporting or refusing to support major party candidates. Among these have been the Farmer-Labor party in Minnesota, the Conservative and the Liberal parties in New York, and the Progressive party in Wisconsin.

Name _____ Date _____

Challenges

1. Who were the two major party candidates in 1968?

_____

_____

2. Which one was hurt most by the Wallace campaign?

_____

3. What was Wallace trying to do?

_____

_____

4. What were some things that Populists wanted that became law?

_____

_____

_____

5. Why didn't the Populists run a candidate in 1896?

_____

_____

6. What nickname was given to Theodore Roosevelt's Progressive party in 1912?

_____

7. Who led the revolt against the two-party system in 1992? What percentage of the popular vote did he get?

_____

_____

8. Why are those who agree with the third parties unwilling to support them with their votes?

_____

_____

9. What types of parties want to destroy the free enterprise system?

_____

_____

10. What category does the Prohibition party fit in?

_____

_____

Name _____ Date _____

Points to Consider

1. What would be a third party's chances if it did not have a dynamic leader on the ticket?

_____

_____

_____

_____

_____

2. What makes people angry with government today? Do you think enough of them are angry about the same things that they would form a third party?

_____

_____

_____

_____

_____

3. Do you think that the minor parties serve any purpose?

_____

_____

_____

_____

_____

Activity

Have the class discuss this issue. As a group concerned about gambling (or some other issue), what problems would they have in convincing others to support their anti-gambling, minor-party candidate?

Who Runs?

In one small town, no one had filed for the office of mayor by the time the deadline had passed. A group of business owners met at a café and decided that a woman who owned a shop in town would make a fine mayor. Word soon spread around town to vote for her. To keep her from protesting, no one told her. When the ballots were counted, she was the unanimous choice; then she was told. She did not complain but laughed with good humor. She was an excellent mayor, serving several terms.

In much the same way, George Washington had no desire to leave his life as a farmer, but all the electors picked him as their choice for president. He said he knew now how the man felt on his way to be executed. These were cases of the job seeking the person. Most people who become officeholders are not picked that way. They have to have the urge to do it, and then they go through the processes of filing, campaigning, and winning.

Since there are so many public offices filled by elections, and they range from unpaid local jobs on school boards to prestigious jobs like governor and president, there is no single motive that causes someone to campaign for public office. The following list includes a few of the reasons that cause men and women to seek public office.

1. THEY SEE A NEED. She sees a need for more books in the school library, so a parent decides to run for school board. He wants more streets paved, so a citizen runs for alderman to correct the problem. There is no desire to gain anything from it but a better school or streets.

Many public offices pay nothing or so little that their paycheck is only enough to complicate their income tax. There is little glory and much sacrifice in their jobs. They will sit through long meetings and endure much criticism and angry phone calls because they want to improve something.

2. ANGER. They are angry at the way crime is growing, schools are being run, or government is failing to do something they think is important. They blame the problems on the people in office and think they can clean up the mess in city hall or the capitol.

In the early 1900s, a group called the Progressives, made up of middle-class reformers, began running for office and making changes that included primary elections, better schools, more parks, better water and sewer systems, and civil service tests for government employees.

3. PRESTIGE. There is some appeal to being important. Being addressed as "Your honor" or "Senator," having the attention of crowds, and having the special privileges of office attracts certain people.

4. FINANCIAL REWARD. They need a job or want to make the higher salary the political office pays.

5. POWER. They like to be at the center of the action. They want to be the one making decisions, giving commands, and doing great things.

6. DUTY. Some families have traditions of being involved in public service. In an earlier time this was called *noblesse oblige* [no-bles o-blezh] . This meant that a person in a position of wealth or privilege had a duty to serve the public. Many early leaders of the United States felt this sense of duty. Washington, Adams, Franklin, and Jefferson often took jobs with little or no pay.

If there are reasons why people want to be elected, there are also reasons why they do not want to run.

1. TIME. It takes much time to get elected. Ringing door bells, shaking hands, listening to everyone's opinions, giving talks, studying issues, and perhaps even debating are all time-consuming. The candidate misses out on leisure and family activities. Some people do not want to sacrifice the time.

2. JOB. It is harder for people in some occupations to run or hold office. Their work hours may interfere with the duties of the job. If they run a business that takes too much time, they cannot do it.

3. THEY MAY NOT FEEL QUALIFIED. Those with little education often feel they do not know enough to handle the job.

4. VIEWS. The person's views on issues may keep them from running. The community may be against raising taxes, but he is in favor of major improvements on the school. The town may be an "X" Party stronghold, and he is a member of the "Y" Party. As one writer put it: "A man ain't got no right to be a public man, unless he meets the public views."

5. PRIVACY. When a person runs for public office, his or her whole life becomes the subject of discussion. Anything, no matter how trivial, can be brought out by the opponent, and some candidates would much prefer accusing the opponent of some wrong occurring 20 years before than talk about their own records over the last two years.

Jefferson wrote that "when a man assumes a public trust, he should consider himself as public property." The prying eyes of the press into the most minor details of an office-holder and his or her family and friends today goes far beyond anything Jefferson had in mind. Many well-qualified people feel there is too much attention to the private life to suit them.

6. CRITICISMS OF PUBLIC OFFICIALS. Accusations that politicians are corrupt and untruthful are often heard. One writer said that a politician will "doublecross that bridge when he comes to it." Artemus Ward wrote in 1859: "I'm not a politician and my other habits are good."

A person who enters politics can be honest. Many in public life admit there are many pressures to tell half-truths and take popular shortcuts, but it can be done. John Kennedy said: "Public officials are not a group apart. They reflect the moral tone of the society in which they live."

7. CONFIDENCE IS LACKING. They do not think they are rich, smart, or good-looking enough to win an election, or they do not think they could do the job if they were elected.

Name _____ Date _____

Challenges

Each statement below matches which motive for running (by name)?

1. The mayor's job pays twice as much as mine, and I'm as smart as he is.

_____

2. In my 10 years on the city council, I've never seen a mayor mess up like this one has. I could do better than he has.

_____

3. We could use more flowers in the city park.

_____

4. If I were mayor, I'd get better service at that restaurant.

_____

5. I enjoy making things happen. I'll shake everything up at city hall.

_____

Each statement below matches which motive for not running (by name)?

6. There was never an honest politician, and I'm not like that.

_____

7. I don't want flashbulbs popping from bushes at my family barbeques.

_____

8. I favor gun control, and this town is full of deer hunters.

_____

9. How could a teacher like me run for the state legislature when it meets during the school year?

_____

10. I barely have time to sit down for dinner now.

_____

Name _____ Date _____

Points to Consider

1. Why do some people seem to be natural leaders, and everyone thinks they should be political leaders?

_____

_____

_____

_____

_____

_____

2. Do you think that one person can make a difference in making government run better? Why?

_____

_____

_____

_____

_____

_____

3. Which reasons for not running are more likely to be honest, and which are usually just excuses?

_____

_____

_____

_____

_____

_____

Activity

Have the class research the background of people in public life and try to discover what caused them to run for office.

Who Votes?

In 1948, all the polls indicated that Thomas Dewey was going to win the presidential election by a large margin. As the returns came in, some of the most important newscasters said: "Truman is ahead now, but when the final votes are counted, Dewey will win." The Chicago *Tribune* went to press early, and its headline announced Dewey's victory. But Dewey did *not win,* and many people had trouble explaining why they had been so wrong.

Politics is a game where there are rules, but there is always the possibility of a surprise upset. Many who thought they did not have to worry because they had won easily before have found themselves out of office. In this chapter, we look at three questions. Who votes? Which party will they support? How does the question of "who votes" affect the campaign?

WHO VOTES? More than half of voters go to the polls for presidential elections, but in off-year elections, when all House members and many governors and state officials are picked, the turnout is less than 40 percent. Studies show that there are several reasons why someone votes.

1. If they have close ties to a political party, they are more likely to vote. In the 1890s, back before there were cars and voting machines, a larger percentage voted than do now. As party loyalty has declined, the percentage of adults who vote has dropped.

2. Those who feel it is their responsibility as citizens are more likely to vote. They are likely to be middle-aged and older or to have been in the armed services.

3. The better educated more often study the issues and candidates and support the person and party they feel can do the best job.

4. Whites are more likely to vote than African-Americans. Voting is a habit that is not as well developed in some minority groups.

5. A close election will bring out more voters. Because of the emphasis on the presidential race, this helps the party of the more popular presidential candidate and hurts the less popular opponent's party. In 1956, Eisenhower's popularity was so high that everyone knew who would win before the election took place, and only 61 million voted. The 1960 election between Kennedy and Nixon was hard-fought, and no one knew who would win; 68 million voted in that election.

6. An important issue will create interest in the election. In 1964, many citizens feared that Barry Goldwater might lead us into World War III, and despite the almost certain victory of Lyndon Johnson, 74 million people voted. Issues vital to a city or state bring out more voters in local elections. Taxes, education, streets, and highways are big issues affecting people's lives and billfolds. In national elections, many issues are discussed. Some attract attention, and others get lost in the confusion. Candidates often look for the issue that will cause voters to support them.

Voters may become excited by an issue, but not always for the same side. For instance, highway users may disagree strongly on whether to raise gasoline taxes for highway improvement. If the issue is a bond issue to build a new elementary school to relieve overcrowding, the parents of young children may encourage people to vote for it, while those who have no children may say taxes are too high now and urge a vote against it.

If no issue attracts much attention, and if the public is satisfied with the way things are, they are less likely to vote. That is the reason the "Y" party tries to bring up the failures of the present "X" administration—to stir up public anger against the "X" party and get the loyal "Y" members to campaign harder. The "X" party assures the public that they have everything under control and that the "Y" party members are just complainers and whiners: "If you want things to keep going well, keep us in power." Campaign advertising for both the "X" and "Y" parties gives an image they are trying to sell to the public. If the economy is good, the streets are safe, and the public is confident of the future, the "X" party benefits.

6. Great enthusiasm for a candidate will encourage a larger voter turnout. Both the "X" and "Y" parties will make their candidates look wonderful. If Candidates "A" and "B" are both exciting, the vote will be larger.

WHICH PARTY WILL THEY VOTE FOR? In almost every partisan election, the votes of some party loyals will not switch. Their votes are secure for Party "X" or "Y." With the percentage of these party loyals declining, however, election support is less sure. The South was once so Democratic it was called the "Solid South," but no more. Some states on the Great Plains and New England were Republican states, but not anymore. States often have pockets of minority party strength, and if that minority finds better candidates and works hard, they can take elected offices away from the complacent majority.

To review, not every group votes in the same numbers. Issues and candidates can arouse enthusiasm, and neither party is assured of victory in any state or section of the country anymore.

HOW VOTING PATTERNS AFFECT CAMPAIGNS. Being a smart candidate, "A" studies the records to see who will *not* vote. Among these are the unemployed, those with poor jobs, those with a grade-school education, those between 18 and 24 years old, and the poor. In Anytown, our first example in the book, Candidate "A," who is running for mayor, does not waste time campaigning in the poorer sections of town where the nonvoters live. He campaigns on issues that appeal to those who will vote. Candidate "A" will promise to repave the streets on Ritzy Hill and provide better police protection for the middle-class sections. To keep the poor people in the Valley from being so angry that they will turn out in large numbers to vote for "B," he promises to gravel their streets, increase the number of city garbage collectors, and mow their park more often.

33

Name _____ Date _____

Challenges

1. Which election is more likely to have the largest turnout, the one in the year 2002 or 2004? Why?

_____

_____

2. Why did a larger percentage vote in the 1890s than do now?

_____

_____

3. How many more people voted in 1960 than in 1956? Why was the turnout so much higher?

_____

_____

4. Which issue do you think will attract more public attention: taxes or global warming? Why?

_____

_____

5. In the example of building a new elementary school, why did parents support it?

_____

_____

6. Why might an elderly person living on Social Security oppose building the school?

_____

_____

7. Which party ruled in the days of the "Solid South"?

_____

8. What parts of the country were once Republican strongholds?

_____

_____

9. Which groups in Anytown would most benefit if Candidate "A" suggested the need for a new golf course and a new terminal at Anytown Airport?

_____

_____

10. Why does Candidate "A" offer to do anything for the poor people of the Valley?

_____

_____

Name _____ Date _____

Points to Consider

1. Why do some issues attract so much attention, and others, which may be just as important, attract so little?

_____

_____

_____

_____

_____

2. Why are some candidates so much more appealing than others?

_____

_____

_____

_____

_____

3. Why might a candidate prefer talking about cutting taxes than costly improvements in highways?

_____

_____

_____

_____

_____

Activity

Discuss "A's" campaign in Anytown. Is it smart politics to favor those who vote over those who do not? Is it the right thing to do?

State and Local Elections

While elections for governor, state legislator, mayor, or sheriff rarely attract national attention, they are of great importance to the citizens involved.

The elections for state and local officials vary widely: state requirements for filing, whether the population is urban or widely scattered, the size of the population, cost of the campaign, and importance the public attaches to the office.

A few differences can be quickly discussed by terms that are used.

PARTISAN OR NONPARTISAN. For some jobs, candidates are listed by party labels (partisan), and others are elected without party labels (nonpartisan). Statewide and major city-elected offices are almost always chosen in partisan elections. Nonpartisan elections are those where the people think political labels are not desirable; these include most school boards and elected officials of many small towns.

LOCAL OFFICES are those limited to city and county government and independent special districts. Cities normally elect mayors and aldermen (they represent wards in the city). They pass ordinances (city laws), appoint department heads, and decide how city tax money is to be spent.

County boards have different titles depending on the state, but they are often called *commissioners* or *supervisors.* They have many of the same responsibilities for rural areas in the county that a council does for the city. Other county officials are elected separately and work with the county board. These include the *clerk* (usually handles elections, issues licenses, and keeps county records), *recorder* (records land titles and deeds and keeps legal documents that the state requires), *prosecuting attorney* (prosecutes those accused of crimes within the county), and the *sheriff* (arrests those suspected of crimes and runs the county jail).

Most school districts elect board members in nonpartisan elections. The board has limits set by the state in such areas as how much they can tax, courses required, and building safety.

Special districts provide a particular service like ambulance service, levee and fire protection, parks, water supply, libraries, and hospitals. These each have separate boards and may go beyond county lines.

STATE OFFICES. The governors and state legislators are all elected. Many important state officials are appointed by the governor with the approval of the state senate, but other jobs are often filled by election. Among these are the *secretary of state* (keeps state records and charters corporations), *attorney-general* (the state's official lawyer), and the *treasurer* (pays the state's bills). Some states also elect many state boards.

If there are also other referendums and initiative questions on the ballot, the voter has many choices to make in a few minutes at the polls.

WHY DO WE ELECT SO MANY OFFICIALS? The reason for choosing so many officeholders resulted from a suspicion that political leaders were appointing unqualified friends and dishonest supporters to jobs. The best solution for that was to make the job an elected one and let voters do the selecting. Voting on constitutional amendments and initiative petitions were added because the public did not trust the legislature to make decisions that might limit their own powers.

SHORT BALLOTS. Some states use "short ballots" that list fewer offices to be elected. The "long ballot" is used in other states. It gives the voters many offices to fill.

With all of these jobs to fill and important questions to answer, problems have been created for those running for office and the voters.

1. If "A" and "B" from the "X" party decide to run for the same office, they compete in the primary. That costs money and may cause arguments between party members that may cause some to vote for the "Y" candidate. Meanwhile, "C" is the only candidate running on the "Y" ticket. "A" has to spend most of his limited funds to defeat "B," while "C" still has his money and can use all of it for the general election. Even if "A" wins the primary and is far better qualified than "C," "C" might win the general election because of the publicity he can buy.

2. Candidates have a hard time raising money for their campaigns. If "D" is running for the job of county clerk, friends may help fund the campaign, but it is almost certain his or her party will not help. Voters have little information on the qualifications of candidates because of this.

3. Some races draw wide attention and others almost none. The races for governor, sheriff, and mayor attract wide attention in the state, county, and city, but other races may be almost ignored. This leaves the voter with the choice of leaving the ballot blank, going by political party, going by name recognition, or guessing. Some voters simply vote for president and a few other offices and leave the rest of the ballot blank.

4. Campaigns for governor, U. S. Senate, and House seats are very expensive and require the spending of hundreds of thousands of dollars. Part of this money is raised by parties and candidates from individuals, but part of it comes from businesses, unions, and political action committees (PACs) that want to influence officeholders. Some argue that tax money should be used to finance campaigns and no private funds should be allowed. They say that too many elections are bought, not won.

5. Political parties have little control over who runs on their ticket. That can be embarrassing if the candidate is nutty, has a bad reputation, or has views that differ from those the party represents. Sometimes, the party leaders work against their party candidate for that reason.

John Kennedy said that "no government is better than the men who compose it." If we want better government, we need to think about the ways in which we choose our leaders.

Name _____ Date _____

Challenges

1. In a partisan election, how are candidates listed?

_____

_____

2. Are school board elections usually partisan or nonpartisan?

_____

_____

3. Which county official is most likely to attract public attention: the prosecutor or the county recorder? Why?

_____

_____

4. Which county official usually prepares ballots before elections?

_____

_____

5. How do special districts differ from county boards?

_____

_____

6. Why do many states let voters decide on constitutional amendments?

_____

_____

7. Why is it better to be the only candidate running on your party's ticket?

_____

_____

8. What city election draws the most attention?

_____

_____

9. Who, besides individuals, often gives to the more visible campaigns?

_____

_____

10. How much control does the party have over who runs on its ticket?

_____

_____

Name _____ Date _____

Points to Consider

1. Why are city and county governments important to the citizen?

_____

_____

_____

_____

_____

_____

2. Why do you think some races are carried on by television ads, while others are often conducted with shaking hands and ringing bells?

_____

_____

_____

_____

_____

_____

3. List the advantages and disadvantages of the short ballot.

_____

_____

_____

_____

_____

Activity

There are many differences between the general election process discussed in this chapter and some state and local elections. Have the students research how your state, county, or city may be different, and why.

Running for Congress

Before we discuss running for Congress, you need to understand a few basic facts. The Constitution provides for Congress to have two houses: the Senate and House of Representatives. Senators are to have a six-year term; they must be at least 30 years old, a resident of the state that elects him or her, and at least nine years a citizen of the United States. Representatives must be at least 25 years old, a resident of their state, and at least seven years a citizen of the United States. Senators were chosen by the state legislatures at first, but after the Seventeenth Amendment was ratified in 1913, they were chosen by the voters.

Two more Senators are added when a new state is admitted, and the Senate has grown from 26 members in 1789 to 100 senators today. In the first House, there were 65 members, but over time it grew to 435 members. In 1922, the House decided that was big enough, and a law was passed limiting the House to that number. House members now represent about 525,000 people.

Most of the election rules have been set by the states. All senators are chosen by state-wide elections, and members of the House are chosen by districts (except in small states with only one delegate). The Supreme Court ruled that the districts must be nearly equal in population, but the legislatures draw the boundaries for the districts. This has created some strange-looking districts when the legislature has tried to benefit one or the other of the parties. This is called *gerrymandering.* Filing dates and primary rules are set by states, and federal election law requires reports on campaign finance.

HOUSE RACES. There are many differences between House races in the area, the variety of economic interests, racial and ethnic makeup, cost of advertising, and issues affecting the area. To discuss our House race, we will create our own circumstances. Our candidate, "A," has served in the state legislature and is well-known in part of the district. "A" has decided to run against the incumbent, "B," who has been in the House 10 years.

"B" has several advantages over "A"; he or she is known around the whole district, has the *franking privilege* (the right to send mail free), and serves on a committee important to many in the district. "B" takes credit whenever a federal grant is given for sewers or public housing in the district. "B" has built a large campaign fund through donations from special interests. But "B" has certain weaknesses; "B's" record is not outstanding, and "B's" name was recently mentioned in a scandal. "B's" party is not as popular now, and "A's" friends think this is the time to challenge "B."

"A" files with the state to run against "B," and now "A" must organize a campaign. Among the staff "A" may have are a campaign manager, publicity chairman, treasurer, pollster, and researcher. The campaign manager is in charge of staff and volunteers. The publicity person tries to get free television exposure and newspaper articles and develops newspaper ads and commercials. The pollster takes public opinion samples and tries to discover the public's attitudes on issues. The treasurer must account for all money that comes in and fills out financial reports. The researcher studies "B's" record to find any unpopular positions he has taken and helps "A" prepare for any discussion of issues that might come up. If "A" has enough money, "A" may hire a professional consulting firm to help with his or her image.

The campaign will take many hours of work. It will involve giving speeches, shaking hands, attending party rallies, organizing mailing campaigns, and talking to people of all ages. "A" will usually begin with an early breakfast and end with a late-night staff conference.

There will be moments of anger and frustration, but several things will probably inspire "A": the desire to see programs "A" supports become law, anger at charges "B" is making, family and friend enthusiasm, endorsements received from groups and individuals, and the sheer pleasure of the contest. As the race comes to a close, "A" is pumped up, working harder than ever, and trying to convince more people they should support the cause.

Then, it is all over, and win or lose, "A" will know he or she tried.

SENATE RACES are even more complex than House races. Potential candidates often begin to "test the waters," seeing if they can develop voter interest. They begin crisscrossing the state, giving speeches to clubs and at political events and looking for opportunities to get free coverage in newspapers and on talk radio and television. Because of the importance of the office, there are more likely to be primary contests. The candidate will compete against others who may be similar in background and views; somehow, "C" must show ways in which she is more qualified and the better choice. "C" wins the primary in her party, "D" in his.

Unlike the smaller House district, the state has a broader variety of interests, and "C" needs to become acquainted with the needs of factory workers, white-collar employees, farmers, women, large and small business owners, and issues facing education, the elderly, and so on. Foreign trade or immigration may be major issues in the state, and "C" needs to prepare positions on these issues.

Campaigns in large states can be very expensive, and the struggle to keep financial support coming in bothers "C" and "D." There are some who will contribute if the candidate promises to support their group's interests when he or she wins. For many candidates, this is a perplexing problem, and the temptation is strong to trade a favor for a big donation.

Scheduling is a serious problem for the candidates. They cannot spend all their time in big cities or they will lose the rural areas. If the state is large, travel time has to be carefully studied. By November, they are hoarse and exhausted. Election day finally arrives.

The hard work will pay off for one; he or she will be addressed as "Senator." The other will rest awhile, then start looking for a job.

Name _____ Date _____

Challenges

1. How old must a Senator and Representative be?

_____

_____

2. How many Representatives are there now? Who decided on that number?

_____

_____

3. What is gerrymandering?

_____

_____

4. What is the franking privilege?

_____

_____

5. What is the duty of the campaign manager?

_____

_____

6. What does the pollster do?

_____

_____

7. What does "testing waters" mean?

_____

_____

_____

8. Why do Senate races often require a study of more issues than House races?

_____

_____

9. Why might a candidate not want to accept money from some contributors?

_____

_____

10. What is the final reward for a Senate candidate?

_____

_____

Name _____ Date _____

Points to Consider

1. What are some reasons why you think a person decides to run for Congress?

_____

_____

_____

_____

_____

2. Do you think the incumbent always has the advantage?

_____

_____

_____

_____

_____

3. What would be the advantages of trying for a candidate, even if he or she loses the election?

_____

_____

_____

_____

_____

Activity

Look at a map of your state or congressional district. Have students decide what issues would be most important in an election in your state or district. Compare these with issues that might be important in another part of the country.

Running for President

One president asked: "What is there about this place [White House] that anyone would want to get into it?" Another described the White House as a prison. A third found the presidency brought "nothing but drudgery and daily loss of friends." Despite all the responsibilities and the unfair criticism a president receives, many people in public life dream of becoming president and work hard to win the title.

Those who have that ambition face an enormous task. If running for mayor is like putting a 1,000-piece jigsaw puzzle together, and running for senator is like a 10,000-piece puzzle, then running for president is like a 100,000-piece puzzle without a box cover to guide you. No other campaign in the world requires as many people, demands as much organization, and puts as many demands on the candidate as this contest. Yet, before each election, 10 or 12 politicians will announce they are running for the office. Only two will receive major-party nominations, but which two?

The Constitution requires only that the president be at least 35 years old, a natural born citizen (a citizen from birth), and 14 years of residence in the United States. Most Americans fit these qualifications.

Beyond those broad qualifications, there are other qualifications that the public considers. Most who have been major-party candidates have been in Congress, governors of large states, or well-known generals. Business leaders, Cabinet members, and former vice presidents have also been chosen. Only four have been closely related to a former president: John Quincy Adams (son), George W. Bush (son), Benjamin Harrison (grandson), and Franklin Roosevelt (nephew). Some candidates have been governors of smaller states: Franklin Pierce (New Hampshire), Jimmy Carter (Georgia), and Bill Clinton (Arkansas). Only two have won without competition: George Washington and James Monroe. A few had never been elected to public office before: Zachary Taylor, Ulysses Grant, William Howard Taft, and Dwight Eisenhower. In 2008, Barack Obama was the first African-American to be nominated for the presidency by a major party. No woman has received a major-party presidential nomination, but Geraldine Ferraro (1984) and Sarah Palin (2008) were picked to be vice-presidential nominees, and Hillary Clinton made a strong run for the presidential nomination in 2008.

QUALITIES OF SUCCESSFUL CANDIDATES vary, but three stand out.

1. It helps if individuals have done something noteworthy. They may have been a hero, a leader in Congress, or in the headlines frequently. This gives them *name recognition*. People know who they are.

2. They have an ambition for the job or have been urged to run for president by many important people. The urge is strong in some leaders to reach for the highest office in the land. They may feel they have stronger qualities of leadership than any of the others being considered.

3. They have a vision for the nation and are convinced they are the only ones to carry it out. Nixon said: "It is not because the presidency offers a chance to be somebody, but because it offers the chance to do something." They may feel strongly about some is-

sue that all other candidates are ignoring. In 1976, for instance, President Carter felt that government needed an outsider to clean up the mess. In 1980, Ronald Reagan blamed inflation and unemployment on too much government.

After announcing that they are candidates and setting up their campaign committees, the candidates now compete in that maze of contests called caucuses and primaries. Their purpose is to choose delegates to send to the party's national convention. Candidate "E" and other candidates work hard to have delegates friendly to themselves chosen.

A CAUCUS is a meeting to decide which candidate to support. In some states, party leaders make that choice. Iowa's caucus begins with meetings held in homes and ends with a state caucus to choose delegates to the national convention.

PRIMARIES come in a wide variety. *Closed primaries* are limited to registered party members. *Open primaries* allow voters to decide which party primary they will vote in; the voter may have no party or even belong to the opposing party. In some primaries, delegates for each candidate are listed; in some, voters choose from a list of names.

In some states, not only do voters decide on delegates, but there are *preferential primaries* in which the list of candidates is included, and the voter picks his or her favorite. These are often called "beauty contests." If "E" gets 50 percent of the votes, "F" gets 30 percent, and "G" gets 20 percent, the state delegation to the national party convention is split: 50 percent "E" delegates, 30 percent "F," and 20 percent "G." Their support for the candidate may be required only on the first ballot, and after that, they may switch. The primary system is confusing and ever changing. Candidates who look strong at the beginning are called "contenders" by the press, and soon, others begin to drop out. By the time of the convention, only one or perhaps two of those who started the primary trail remains in the running for the nomination.

THE NATIONAL CONVENTION is the gathering place of the party faithful. If "E" has the nomination sewn up, it may be a pep rally to stir up enthusiasm for the general election. Before primaries were established, state parties often chose "favorite sons" to give prominent politicians from the state or region national recognition. At some conventions, contests between the leading contenders are bitter, and the convention ends up choosing a "dark horse," someone who had not been mentioned often before. The 1924 Democratic convention battled through 103 ballots before choosing Judge Alton Parker. In the "X" party convention, "E" wins the nomination and prepares to battle the "Y" party candidate, "F," in the presidential race.

"E" then tries to heal the wounds caused by bitter primary battles. Some of the losing candidates and their supporters will forgive and forget because they cannot support the "Y" candidate. At times, however, there has been so much hostility among the losers that they switched to the other party. The next test is greater and far tougher: winning the grand prize, the title of President.

Name _____ Date _____

Challenges

1. What is the youngest a president can be?

_____

2. Name three presidents who have been close relatives of former presidents.

_____

_____

_____

3. Which two presidents won without having any serious competition?

_____

_____

4. Why did Jimmy Carter want to be president?

_____

_____

5. Why did Ronald Reagan want to be president?

_____

_____

6. Who votes in a closed primary?

_____

_____

7. Who votes in an open primary?

_____

_____

8. In a winner-take-all primary, whoever gets the most votes wins. In a preferential primary, if a candidate gets 60 percent of the vote, what percentage of the delegates do they receive?

_____

9. What happens to candidates who do poorly in the first primaries?

_____

_____

10. What is a "dark horse"?

_____

_____

Name _____ Date _____

Points to Consider

1. Do you think it is likely that someone who does *not* want to be president will ever be chosen again? Why?

_____

_____

_____

_____

_____

_____

2. In the early nineteenth century, candidates were chosen by a caucus of the party leaders. Why do you think the convention system developed?

_____

_____

_____

_____

_____

_____

3. Do you think national conventions are necessary when primaries have often chosen the candidate before the convention is held?

_____

_____

_____

_____

_____

_____

Activity

Request a film from the national parties of their last conventions. Ask the students to study the convention from the view of real enthusiasm and its ability to bring out issues.

Organizing the Presidential Campaign

When "E" is assured the party nomination, his or her next task will be to choose a vice-presidential running mate. Most choose one who will "balance" the ticket. If the nominee is a liberal, "E" might pick a conservative for vice president, or vice versa. If "E" is from the east coast, a west-coast running mate will help. The choice of vice president, in other words, needs to be a candidate who will win support from voters who might not be enthused about the presidential candidate. "E" does not want someone who will disagree with him on issues or might embarrass him in public appearances.

After the conventions, the exhausted candidates of "X" and "Y" parties rest a few days and prepare for the final test: winning in November. In many ways, the campaign organization is in place, but it is not uncommon for the candidate to replace some of the staff at this point. Some of those who were staff to other party candidates in the primaries may have done a better job than the candidate's own staff and are now willing to join the winner's team.

ISSUES. Candidates may also review their positions on issues. For example, "E" knew how party members felt about immigration, and whenever he was asked about his position, he expressed opinions that appealed to them. National polls show, however, that most people disagree with that position. He must decide whether to continue supporting an unpopular position, or he might "explain" that his views have been misquoted. Either approach carries a risk. Those supporting "E" before will be angry if he changes, and the public may vote against "E" if he does not.

A foreign policy crisis may come up during the campaign. If the candidate is from the "X" party, a new issue may develop; if the president is from the "Y" party, "E" will be asked whether he supports the president. "E" might argue that the president is wrong, he might disagree with the way the president is handling the situation, or he might support the president's policies.

Every presidential candidate wants to pick issues that will bring them votes and center around those issues. In 1992, a sign hung at one party's headquarters saying: "It's the economy, stupid." This is often called "setting the agenda." Sometimes, whoever sets the agenda wins.

The presidential and vice-presidential candidates will spend many hours going over issues they have never thought of before and deciding how to respond to them. A position on an issue that is popular with one group or in one part of the country may cost votes somewhere else. What farmers want might not go well with city dwellers. A promise benefiting one state may cost votes in another. Some candidates have found it tempting to give vague answers that make both sides feel he or she favors them.

DEBATES. In 1858, two Illinois candidates competed for the right to become Senator. The Lincoln-Douglas debates became nationally famous, and even though Douglas was chosen, Lincoln became well-known and, two years later, was elected president. Debates between presidential candidates were not held until television became common. Both Richard Nixon and John Kennedy were willing to debate on the "tube" in 1960. No more presidential debates took place until 1976, but they have been a part of presidential campaigns ever since. Vice-presidential candidates have debated since 1984.

Candidates prepare hard for the debates. They go over the facts and have practice sessions with someone standing in for the opponent. A blunder can cost thousands of votes, so they guard against saying something foolish. Each finds ways to exploit the opponent's weaknesses.

Debates have both advantages and problems. The advantages are that the public sees candidates under pressure, and working under pressure is part of the job. We can compare their positions on issues. The problems are that candidates are trying so hard to keep from making a mistake that they give vague answers to the questions. There is also some doubt that the person with the smoothest answers and quickest responses will make the more thoughtful president.

CAMPAIGN SLOGANS sometimes have as much effect as the issues. A good example occurred in 1840, when a Democrat said that the Whig candidate, William Henry Harrison, from the frontier state of Indiana, probably sat on the front porch of his log cabin and drank hard cider. The campaign became known as the "hard cider campaign." The mistake was that many voters lived in log cabins and drank hard cider, so Harrison won. In 1952, a smiling Eisenhower was displayed on campaign buttons with the slogan: "I like Ike." The opposition found that impossible to top.

POLLSTERS are very important to the campaign. Each candidate has a group of staff members who interview many people and ask as many questions as possible. They want to know what issues are most important to people and how the public would respond to different possible solutions. If a person says he or she is disturbed about drugs, the person is asked if he or she favors longer prison time for dealers, more federal money going to police departments to fight drugs, drug treatment programs, or some other solution. If there is a public response that drug dealers should be shot at sunrise, the candidate might offer the "Sunrise Law" if he or she is elected.

STAFFING THE CAMPAIGN. Some candidates prefer having paid staff to using volunteers. The paid worker is more reliable, can probably do the job better, and is not as likely as an overly enthusiastic volunteer to make a blunder that will require "damage control."

On the other hand, there are advantages to using large numbers of volunteers guided by staff. They certainly work cheaper, and there are many jobs they can do as well as paid staff. They will put signs on their own front lawns, will talk to neighbors and friends, and, the day before the election, they will spend the day on the phone to get out the vote. They create part of the excitement that makes a larger turnout possible on election day.

A well-organized campaign puts some pieces of the puzzle together.

Name _____ Date _____

Challenges

1. What is meant by balancing the ticket?

_____

_____

2. Why might the candidate change pollsters between the primaries and the presidential campaign?

_____

_____

3. Is there a difference between what a candidate might say in primaries and what he or she says in the presidential campaign? Why?

_____

_____

4. What does "setting the agenda" mean?

_____

_____

5. Why is deciding where to stand on issues tricky?

_____

_____

6. What was the most famous debate between candidates for Senate?

_____

_____

7. What was the first debate between presidential candidates, and when did it take place?

_____

_____

8. Why do candidates in debates sometimes give vague answers to questions?

_____

_____

9. Why was bringing up the log cabin and hard cider a mistake for the Democrats in 1840?

_____

_____

10. Give two good reasons for using campaign volunteers.

_____

_____

Name _____ Date _____

Points to Consider

1. What are issues that you would like to see candidates bring up in the next election? Would you support a candidate who did not agree with your solutions to these problems?

_____

_____

_____

_____

_____

2. The "Y" party candidate refuses to debate the "X" candidate. Do you think that is a good reason not to support "Y"? Why?

_____

_____

_____

_____

_____

3. Why might a person want to volunteer to help in the campaign of his or her favorite candidate?

_____

_____

_____

_____

_____

Activity

Create a debate topic on an issue facing your community or state. Have the class make a list of different positions that might be taken on that issue. Who would favor each position, and who would oppose it?

Teachers: This chapter may be best suited for advanced students.

Financing the Campaign

Many candidates enjoy campaigning. They like the thrill of a large cheering crowd and seeing their names in headlines. The issues they discuss are exciting to them, and they want to talk about them. The long hours and a different hotel room every night do not bother them. They meet many interesting people along the way, and they enjoy conversations with other political leaders. But one part of being a candidate bothers many of them, and that is asking for contributions.

The candidate knows that without money, there will be no advertising, no staff, and no campaign. It will be all over, and he or she will be a loser. Asking for money is part of running for office, but the candidate knows that some of those who donate want more than your election victory. They will expect you to do favors for them after you win. They may pressure you to vote in favor of policies that favor them or use your influence to get them a government contract. If you do not, their money will probably go to your opponent when you want to be re-elected.

Raising money is a never-ending process for many politicians. They must start gathering campaign funds as soon as the election is over. This upsets many officeholders after a few times, and they retire from public life.

There is an old joke: "How do you get to Carnegie Hall?" The answer is "practice, practice, practice." And how do you become a governor, senator, or president? Unfortunately, a big part of the answer is "money, money, money." This has been part of politics since the 1890s, when big businesses began giving large donations to campaigns in return for favors. Some openly offered bribes to legislators. One business leader took a black bag filled with $500,000 to buy votes in the New York legislature. A writer charged that 75 of the 90 senators had been bought by special interests. The public was outraged.

The Progressives demanded reforms. That was one reason for creating primaries, so honest voters, not special interests, would choose the candidates. One hundred years later, many are concerned that nothing has changed, and raising money seems more important to winning than a candidate's qualifications and the issues.

In 1972, such large amounts of money poured into the Nixon campaign that secret funds were set up. When the burglars who broke into Democratic headquarters were caught, money from a secret fund was used to pay for their trial lawyers. Public demands that election laws be tightened led to the Federal Election Campaign Act of 1974. It said a presidential candidate could not spend more than $10 million in primaries or $20 million in the general election. Since then, those limits have been raised, but the idea of limiting spending has continued.

Limits were set on how much an individual could give to a candidate's campaign, national parties, and to a nonparty committee (PAC). If the presidential candidate accepted these limits, he was eligible to receive some federal funding for his campaign. The Supreme

52

Court ruled in 1976 that these restrictions were constitutional if the candidate accepted the conditions. However, limiting donations to national parties and PACs violated free speech and political activity.

This created a way around the campaign law; big donors could give to a PAC instead of to the candidate. Money given to "E" is limited by law and is referred to as "hard money." PAC money is not limited, and it is called "soft money." The Friends of Good Government PAC, which supports "E," receives big donations from special interests and uses the money to run commercials praising "E" or a position "E" favors. Some PAC ads may be negative advertising that bitterly attacks opposing Candidate "F."

HOW MUCH MONEY GOES TO PRESIDENTIAL CAMPAIGNS? In 1972, $425 million was spent on the presidential campaign; in 1980, it was up to $1.2 billion; $3 billion was spent in 1992. Changes in the system were proposed after the 1996 election but ran into party bickering in Congress. Both parties accept large contributions of soft money, so nothing has been done.

CONGRESSIONAL CAMPAIGNS have also become quite expensive. In the 1996 campaign, the winner of a Senate contest spent an average of $4.7 million. Races of successful candidates for the House spent an average of $673,700. The Federal Election Commission (FEC) reports that in 1995–96, candidates for the House and Senate received $791 million for their campaigns. About $201 million of that came from PACs. Both parties accept large soft money contributions, and neither is enthused about restricting those gifts. Most money coming from individuals comes from people contributing more than $200.

STATE AND LOCAL CAMPAIGNS also have to be paid for, and some races for governor run into millions of dollars. With hundreds of candidates running at the same time at the national, state, and local levels, there are many candidates trying to get the money for their campaigns.

Among proposals to restrict campaign donations have been the following: outlawing soft money, limiting PAC donations, offering free or low-priced television time to candidates who refuse PAC money, encouraging small contributors with income tax credits, stiff fines for violating campaign finance laws, limits on the amount a Congressional candidate raises outside his or her state or district, and the government paying for the campaign.

Name _____ Date _____

Challenges

1. What is the definition of "bribe"? Was taking $500,000 to influence the New York legislature a bribe? Why?

_____

_____

_____

2. Why did Progressives want to create primaries?

_____

_____

3. What led to the passage of the 1974 Federal Election Campaign Act?

_____

_____

_____

4. According to that law, what was the most a candidate could spend in the primaries and general election?

_____

_____

5. What groups did the Supreme Court say it was all right to give any amount to?

_____

_____

6. What is "hard money"?

_____

_____

7. What is "soft money"?

_____

_____

8. How much did the presidential campaign cost in 1992?

_____

9. How much did winners of House seats spend in 1996?

_____

10. How much did winners of Senate seats spend in 1996?

_____

Name _____ Date _____

Points to Consider

1. Do you think that having primaries choose candidates helped solve the problem of big contributors influencing elections? Why?

_____

_____

_____

_____

_____

_____

2. When the PAC attacks "F," "E" campaign money is not used. Do you think "E" bears some responsibility for untrue statements that are made in PAC television ads?

_____

_____

_____

_____

_____

_____

3. Would you favor limiting campaign spending for House and Senate seats? Why?

_____

_____

_____

_____

_____

Activity

What keeps "E" and "F" from agreeing not to accept soft money? Your class is the "E" campaign committee. Would they favor promising not to accept soft money if "F" would do the same? List reasons for and against.

The Media and Public Opinion Polls

If a presidential candidate has ever come to your town, you have seen that they do not travel alone. In chartered airplanes (if the candidate is flying) or buses (if he or she is moving on land), the candidate is surrounded by an army of Secret Service agents, reporters, and photographers. The press trailing behind the candidate are often referred to as "the pack," and they include reporters from major newspapers, the wire services, and television. Wherever the candidate goes, they are sure to follow. Thousands may gather to hear Candidate "E" speak, but millions will learn what he said in their morning newspapers and on the nightly news.

While the press is doing its work, pollsters are busy trying to figure out which candidate is most popular with the public and what issues are most important. For "E," these groups can make or break his or her efforts.

Coverage of the campaign begins with the early primaries, where 10 or 12 candidates are trying to win the "X" party nomination. The powerful and famous have the advantage at this time, and the media focuses on them. The lesser-known candidates struggle among themselves for a little publicity. There are surprises; leading candidates run out of money or draw small crowds, and someone in the lesser-known group moves up. In 1976, reporters at first paid little attention to Jimmy Carter, a former Southern governor campaigning in New Hampshire. When he won the primary, the press left other candidates and concentrated more on him.

All candidates have press secretaries. It is their job to see that the press is getting favorable impressions about the candidate. They do this through briefings (news conferences), informal chats, and press handouts. The press secretary often arranges hotel rooms and lunches for the media, in the hope they will be in a better mood when they write their articles.

Those who get little coverage usually do poorly in the primaries and have a hard time persuading potential donors to contribute to their campaigns. They begin dropping out, and the few reporters assigned to them move on to cover those remaining. The dropouts blame defeat on the media.

After Richard Nixon lost the presidential election in 1960, he ran for governor of California in 1962 and lost again. He was sure that the reason for his failures was the liberal press. In a famous news conference, he announced that he was dropping out of politics and said: "You won't have Richard Nixon to kick around anymore." He soon returned to politics, winning the presidency in 1968 and 1972. But Nixon was always suspicious of the press, and he preferred talking to a few friendly reporters rather than holding full press conferences. His vice president, Spiro Agnew, often accused the press of biased reporting, and that hurt press relations with Nixon even more. After two reporters found evidence of a

Nixon cover-up of the Watergate break-in, Nixon was pressured by Congress to resign.

The primaries are over, and "E" has won the nomination. Before the presidential contest between "E" and "F" begins, we know that some newspapers are friendly to "E" and will make him look good. Other newspapers will support "F."

The Associated Press (AP), network television, and other news services may try to be fair to "E" and "F," but even their reports may be called "friendly" or "unfriendly" by the candidates. In other words, the candidate falling behind is almost certain to blame it on the media.

Candidates are also critical of the amount of newspaper space and television time devoted to their campaigns. In fairness, there is only so much room on the front page for the presidential campaign, and evening news has only about 24 minutes for *all* the news of the day. If nothing new or exciting has been done by "E" or "F" in the last 24 hours, a minute or two is all the coverage they will get. Candidates learn to make short, profound, or witty quotes so they will be aired.

PUBLIC OPINION POLLS have become a basic part of the campaign. These are being conducted by the candidates and by independent groups like the Gallup and Roper polls.

Candidate polls tell the candidates what is working and what is not. They find the issues that turn the public on and which solutions people favor for those issues. If polls indicate that voters are concerned about the cost of medical care, "E" and "F" are certain to talk about it. The two candidates may disagree on how to reduce costs, and that will be a major topic to be debated. The polls will also cover public attitude toward the candidate and may change their style of campaigning. If "E's" polls report that his speeches are dull, he becomes more dynamic. If he seems like a stuffed shirt, he puts more jokes in his speeches and is photographed in sports shirts.

Independent polling. The big names in independent polling have been Gallup, Roper, and Lou Harris. In recent years, a number of newspaper and network polls have become important. Polling techniques have improved greatly since the 1936 *Literary Digest* poll predicted that Alf Landon would win the election; Landon was defeated 523 to 8 in electoral votes and by 11 million popular votes. The 1948 election was another polling disaster, with Dewey in such a strong lead that no polls were taken during the last two weeks of the campaign. Dewey lost. In 1980, there were so many undecided voters that polls were no help.

The larger the number and the better the cross section of the public polled, the more accurate the results will be.

There are questions about whether polling (1) is accurate, (2) causes candidates to switch positions to suit public opinion, and (3) causes many voters to jump on the bandwagon and switch to a more popular candidate.

Name _____ Date _____

Challenges

1. What is "the pack"?

_____

_____

2. What are the two things pollsters do during the campaign?

_____

_____

3. Why does the press concentrate on better-known candidates?

_____

_____

4. What does the press secretary do to inform the press?

_____

_____

_____

5. Who said to reporters: "You won't have _____ to kick around anymore"?

_____

6. Who was often used by Nixon to attack the press?

_____

7. What does the "AP" stand for that appears at the beginning of many articles in your city's newspaper?

_____

8. How do candidates hope to make the most use of the minute or two they will get on the evening news?

_____

_____

_____

9. What magazine was damaged by its 1936 poll?

_____

10. What threw the polling off in 1948?

_____

_____

Name _____ Date _____

Points to Consider

1. Do all candidates deserve equal coverage? If not, which candidates deserve the most reporters?

_____

_____

_____

_____

_____

_____

2. Do you think that reporters who dislike a candidate can ruin his or her campaign? If they can, should those reporters be assigned to follow it?

_____

_____

_____

_____

_____

_____

3. Should a candidate change his or her mind about an issue when polls show the public disagrees with his or her position?

_____

_____

_____

_____

_____

Activity

As members of "E's" enthusiastic staff, how do you think the staff should deal with those reporters in the pack who write negative articles about "E"?

The Electoral College

At the Constitutional Convention, the delegates quickly decided that a president should lead the executive branch. When they asked how the president was to be chosen, there were many different ideas. Some said that voters should elect the president, but others objected, saying the people were too uninformed to do the choosing. Remember that in 1787, there were few newspapers, and the most famous candidate might get chosen rather than the best. Some thought Congress should pick the president, but that would make the president their servant. They scrapped both ideas and chose a new one, the *electoral college.* Each state would have as many electors as it had seats in the Senate and House. A state with five representatives has seven electors (2 Senators + 5 Representatives). In order to be declared the winner, the nominee had to be chosen by a majority of the electors.

In the early days, electors were chosen by state legislatures, but in the 1830s, voters demanded the right to pick them. The voters pick the electors, who then choose the president. There are 100 Senators and 435 Representatives, a total of 535. In addition, the Twenty-third Amendment gave three electors to the District of Columbia. With 538 electors, it requires 270 to win the election. If no one has a majority, the House chooses the president from the top three candidates. Another thing to keep in mind is that states cast all their votes for the candidate who gets the most votes in the state.

Every 10 years, after the census is taken, the number of electors a state has is changed. Some states lose electors, and others gain them.

It is the electoral college, not popular vote, that runs the presidential election. A candidate would gladly trade a 100,000-vote victory in a state with four electors for a win by 50 votes in a state with 30 electoral votes.

ELECTORAL COLLEGE AND THE CAMPAIGN. "E" and "F" are both looking for victory in the high electoral states like California, New York, Texas, Florida, and so on. The high-count states will get frequent visits from the presidential candidates. Those with medium-sized votes will receive short visits by the presidential candidate on his or her way through to a larger state, but those with small votes and no large neighbors are rarely visited by the presidential candidate. The vice-presidential candidate is sent to smaller cities in big states and to the more isolated small states.

Our imaginary candidate, "E," is from California, and his running mate, "G," is from Pennsylvania. The "Y" party's nominee, "F," is from Florida, and his running mate, "H," is governor of Wisconsin. Normally, the candidates' home states are secure for the two parties. In addition, certain states are loyal "X" states, and others have large "Y" majorities.

Public opinion polls are important in deciding who goes where. Suppose that polls show that Ohio favors "E" by a 6 to 4 margin and Oregon favors "F" by a 7 to 3 margin in mid-October. It is doubtful that an "E" visit will cause Oregonians to vote for him or that a visit by "F" will change Ohio's mind. Why go there when it will change nothing? Candidates write certain states off as won or lost and concentrate on those that are closer.

Polls indicate that the strong Pennsylvania support "E" had when the campaign began has dropped to 52 percent now, and Massachusetts, which had been strongly for "F" in the beginning, is becoming much closer now. This is a good time for "E" to visit Philadelphia and Boston. While "E" is in New England, he also drops in on Connecticut and Rhode Island.

Candidates also raid each other's territories. "F" makes a quick swing through Oregon and Washington. This makes "E" nervous, so he goes to Portland and Seattle instead of making a trip to Illinois. The campaign becomes a game of stealing votes the other side thought were secure.

Candidates can't be everywhere, but they use television news and commercials to their advantage. "E" hopes that a visit to a few farms will show that he is concerned about all farmers. City-bred candidates may even try to milk a cow or have a picture taken seated on a tractor. The younger candidates will have "photo opportunities" talking to residents of a nursing home. Political experts call this "posturing" (assuming an attitude for effect). Some candidates can pull it off, but others simply look foolish.

The location of television commercials is also important to candidates. Before "E" goes to Boston, New England television stations will increase the number of commercials to bring out larger crowds. "Advance men" are sent ahead of "E" to talk with "X" party leaders and groups favoring "E" to get a large crowd together for the parade to Fenway Stadium for the rally. Plans are made for celebrities from local teams and local "X" party candidates to be there for photo opportunities.

Along the way, "E" and "F" are offering promises everywhere. "I will build a dam" here or "start an urban renewal project" there. These are often forgotten once the election is over, but that does not surprise most voters.

To summarize, "E" and "F" are more interested in electoral votes than popular votes. Candidates are constantly on the road reaching as many voters as possible, and where they cannot go, they send television commercials.

THE POPULAR VOTE ISSUE. Critics of the electoral college feel that it is undemocratic. It does not let the voters have the final word. They point out that a victory by close margins in 12 big states would win the election. Voters in the other 38 states might just as well stay home. Two presidents (Rutherford B. Hayes and Benjamin Harrison) were elected with less popular votes than their leading opponent, and in 14 elections, the winner had less than the combined total of other candidates. Constitutional amendments have been offered to change the system but have never received much support.

Why has it not changed? Some say: "If it isn't broke, don't fix it." The system works. States are not excited about changing the system. Big states do not want to lose their influence, and some small states have more effect in electoral votes than they would have in popular vote.

61

Name _____ Date _____

Challenges

1. If a state has 10 House seats, how many electors does it have?

_____

_____

2. Who chose electors in the 1820s?

_____

_____

3. What happens if no one has a majority in the electoral vote?

_____

_____

_____

4. If Candidate "E" got 350 electoral votes, would he want to trade with "F" who had five million more popular votes? Why?

_____

_____

5. Where are vice-presidential candidates usually sent?

_____

_____

6. Why did "F" decide not to go to Ohio?

_____

_____

7. Why did "E" go to Philadelphia?

_____

_____

8. Why would a man who knows nothing about farms milk a cow?

_____

_____

9. What is "posturing"?

_____

_____

10. If a candidate won the right 12 states, would he or she win the election?

_____

_____

Name _____ Date _____

Points to Consider

1. Why did the Convention choose the electoral college method over popular election? Do you think their reasons are still valid?

_____

_____

_____

_____

_____

_____

2. Do you think commercials are a good substitute for having the candidate visit your city?

_____

_____

_____

_____

_____

_____

3. An amendment was offered in Congress that would declare the candidate who gets the most votes the winner, if that person receives at least 40 percent of the votes. Would you support that amendment?

_____

_____

_____

_____

_____

Activity

Have the students look at a map that shows the electoral votes of each state. Then have them prepare a one-week travel schedule for a candidate. They should plan for several stops each day, allowing time for travel and the day's activities.

Expecting the Unexpected

Have you ever seen a basketball game where all the balls went into the hoop or a football game where every play was a touchdown? The coach and players plan for everything to go perfectly, but it does not happen. There are too many players on the other team who are determined to prevent those game plans from working. Even if the opponents stand like statues, shots will miss the hoop, and passes will be dropped.

The same thing happens in political campaigns. The candidate can make brilliant plans, but usually something goes wrong, and everything is thrown off. The campaign is at best an obstacle course, and sometimes it is like a mine field. A mistake at the worst time can ruin everything. The only consolation is that the opponent may stumble worse, and that may save the candidate.

1. FINANCIAL PROBLEMS. There are limits on how much the campaign can raise. If too much is spent early, not enough is left for the last few days of the campaign. Candidates not only have to keep raising money during the campaign, but they have to watch expenses as well. Is it better to hire a political consultant who works for $100,000 or to hire five workers for $20,000 each? Candidates who are far behind struggle to get financial support. In 1896, William Jennings Bryan's campaign was conducted with pennies, desperately short on money, while William McKinley had more money pouring in than he could spend. Harry Truman's 1948 campaign was so starved for money that when his campaign train stopped in Oklahoma, there was no money to continue. Wealthy oil men were invited to meet with the candidate, and they took up a collection. The campaign continued.

2. EMBARRASSMENTS FROM THE PAST. Candidates are "under the microscope" of the press and the opponent. Suddenly, an arrest for drunk driving 20 years before or avoiding the draft become major issues. Another ghost from the past that haunts candidates are votes they have cast or decisions they have made as a legislator or governor. The candidate's family can be an embarrassment if they have had drinking or drug problems or have been involved in questionable business deals.

3. TIMING. The presidential contest lasts for months, and candidates, like any other humans, have limits on how much they can take. Older candidates, like Franklin Roosevelt in 1944, Bob Dole in 1996, and John McCain in 2008, are under pressure to prove they can last four years if they are elected. Roosevelt was slow to start campaigning in 1944, but when he did, he stirred up the crowds as much as ever. Dole set a schedule that wore his young staff members out. If "E" is ahead by a large margin, he is tempted to work harder to make the election a landslide. "F," who is trailing, does not want to go down in history as a big loser. Both risk their health in the contest by not sleeping enough and working too long. They must pace themselves carefully, taking time out to rest up for the last brutal weeks of the campaign.

4. ADVERTISING in campaigns is as important as it is to car companies. Some ad campaigns have been very effective, even if they have not always been fair. The "daisy girl" commercial in 1964 was a classic example. Taking advantage of public worry that Barry Goldwater's rashness might start World War III, the Democrats put out a commercial showing a girl picking flowers while a voice ticked off a countdown from 10 to one. An atomic blast was seen, and a warning followed: "These are the stakes...[and] the stakes are too high for you to stay home." On the black screen are the words: "Vote for President Johnson on November 3." The commercial was only shown once, but it caught the nation's attention.

Some ads may reach one audience, but they may anger others. For example, "E's" ad supporting clean air might appeal to an environmentalist, but it might lose the vote of a worker whose job would be lost if air standards were tightened.

5. NON-CAMPAIGN EVENTS. A big murder story, a riot, a major flood or earthquake, or some other event at home or abroad may pop up during the campaign and bump stories about the candidates off the front page. After Martin Luther King, Jr. was arrested in1960 during civil rights protests, Vice President Richard Nixon said nothing, but Robert Kennedy, brother of Senator John Kennedy, sent a message of support to King. African-American enthusiasm for Kennedy rose, and that helped him win.

The presidential campaign usually slows down during a major event like the World Series or when important football games are being played. Some events can be anticipated, but others cannot.

6. THE OPPONENT. The campaign is like a sporting event, and you not only have to plan what you are going to do, but you must also watch what the opponent is doing. Your plans may have to be switched because of moves he or she is making.

7. BLOOPERS are stupid mistakes, and they often come toward the end of the campaign. "E" and "F" are both exhausted and get little sleep. Their minds are less sharp now, and they may say the wrong thing, stumble from a platform, or lose their temper at the wrong time. They may forget which city they are in after a long trip, or they may not remember the name of the governor or senator standing beside them on the platform. Candidates become cautious. To prevent errors, "E" repeats the same script he has used for the last few days. He hopes that "F" is more tired than he is, and a blunder by "F" will cause the public to reject "F" and rush to "E's" side.

When election night finally comes, most candidates sit in a hotel room watching the results come in with a few friends. Some watch early returns and go to bed early. By morning, a winner has usually been declared, and the final act of the campaign takes place. The winner goes into a happy, excited crowd, and they all feel the joy of victory. The loser stands before a dejected crowd, thanks them for their support, and offers congratulations to the victor. The campaign is over for now, but in four years, it will be repeated as it has for over 200 years.

Name _____ Date _____

Challenges

1. What are two examples of campaigns short on money?

_____

_____

2. What was meant by "under the microscope"?

_____

_____

_____

3. How are the campaigns of Roosevelt in 1944, Dole in 1996, and McCain in 2008 similar?

_____

_____

4. Why does "E" work harder when he or she is well ahead?

_____

_____

5. Why does "F" work harder when he or she is far behind?

_____

_____

6. What fear did the "daisy girl" commercial use to its advantage?

_____

_____

7. How did Robert Kennedy help his brother's campaign by supporting Dr. King?

_____

_____

8. What is the effect of the World Series on the campaign?

_____

_____

9. What is a "blooper"?

_____

_____

10. How do candidates try to avoid making bloopers?

_____

_____

Name _____ Date _____

Points to Consider

1. Why might a candidate who is behind take more risks than one who is ahead?

_____

_____

_____

_____

_____

2. As a candidate planning a rally at an outdoor stadium, list several things that could go wrong.

_____

_____

_____

_____

_____

_____

3. How do you think you would react at the end of a hard campaign?

_____

_____

_____

_____

_____

Activity

Some compare a political campaign to a game. Taking some popular sports and games, what similarities do students see between them and a campaign?

What Does It Take to Win?

If there were a magic potion that could bring certain victory to a candidate, there would be no shortage of customers eager to buy it. When Anytown School holds its student council elections, Bill tries to win by friendship, and Laura tries to win by providing pizza. Only one of the two will get elected, and some will be inclined to say that friends or bribes win elections, but what works in one classroom will fail in another.

There are certain qualities that seem important in success.

1. DRIVE. You have to want the job, and if you don't want it enough, there are plenty of reasons to get discouraged and quit. Many of those who announce they will run for office find the race too hard and find a reason to drop out. The jobs at the top in the state or federal government are filled with ambitious people who may have been defeated before but kept on anyway. Andrew Jackson was defeated in the 1824 presidential race, but he was elected in 1828. Lincoln was defeated for the Illinois Senate seat in 1858, but he became president in 1860. Grover Cleveland lost his job as president in 1888, but he regained it in 1892. Franklin Roosevelt ran for vice president in 1920, and lost; in 1932, he won the presidency. Richard Nixon lost the presidential election of 1960, but he won in 1968. Ronald Reagan lost the battle to be the Republican nominee in 1976, but he was nominated and won in 1980.

2. CHARISMA is defined as a "special quality of leadership that captures the imagination." Some presidents have had it: Washington, Jackson, both Roosevelts, Eisenhower, Kennedy, and Reagan among them. Your state has probably had some governors who have had that special charm.

This charm gives them what politicians call "availability." That is, they are the ones most likely to be considered when the party is looking at candidates for high offices. It is not the only consideration, however. Some who are quiet and unassuming have also climbed the ladder to success, but with hard work, not personality. Among presidents who have risen this way were John Quincy Adams, James Madison, William H. Taft, Calvin Coolidge, and Harry Truman.

3. INTELLIGENCE. An ability to understand issues and express oneself in a clear way is an asset to someone who wants to get into politics. The more you read, the more you think, and the better you write and speak, the more likely you are to be successful at whatever you want to do. In politics, these skills are especially important.

If you are a presidential candidate, there is no end of issues that you will be asked about: environment or cloning (science), cyberspace (technology), international trade or business issues (economics), family or racial issues (sociology), war policies (military), health care (medicine), and so on. You will even be asked questions about sports, and you will lose votes fast if you cannot tell a home run from a touchdown.

4. GOOD TIMING. A person who might be ignored as a candidate at one time may be exactly what the people are looking for in another. In 1928, the United States was a picture of prosperity. Factories were busy, and unemployment barely existed. People called it "Republican prosperity." The Republican, Herbert Hoover, easily won. By 1932, the economy was in terrible shape, and most Americans blamed it on Hoover. Franklin Roosevelt was the Democratic nominee, and he easily won. The economy was a big part of both elections. One time it helped Republicans, the next time, Democrats. If Roosevelt had run in 1928, he would have lost, but waiting for the right time helped. Public opinion changes on many things, including politics. The liberal so popular in one election may be replaced by someone more conservative in the next election.

5. POLITICAL SKILLS. Politics was defined by Otto Von Bismark as "the art of the possible," and by Harold Laswell as knowing "who gets What, When, How." In democracies, it is knowing how to please the public and work with other officeholders. Lyndon Johnson was by all accounts a persuasive person who hit Washington like a storm when he came as an assistant to a Congressman in the 1930s. His ability to convince people in private conversations was a key to his success. Others are very persuasive in speeches; good examples have been the Roosevelts, Kennedy, and Reagan.

6. LUCK has always been a secret ingredient affecting American politics, and it would be hard to explain our history without involving people who were at the right place at the right time.

A minister from America shopped in a store in the West Indies and met a bright young clerk. The minister arranged for the clerk to go to college in the American colonies. The young man's name was Alexander Hamilton, founder of the Federalist party. Patrick Henry had failed at both farming and business; in desperation, he became a lawyer and leader in the protests against English rule.

Andrew Jackson was elected a general in the Tennessee militia by one vote, the first step on his way to the White House. Lincoln was fortunate enough to lose the election for senator in 1858; two years later, he was elected president. Wilson was a struggling university president in 1910 when his party suggested he run for governor of New Jersey. Two years after he became governor, he was elected president. If Truman's men's clothing store had been more successful, he might not have been so interested when the opportunity came to run for the county judge (term then used in Missouri at the time for county commissioner). Lyndon Johnson was elected to the Senate by an 87-vote majority; he was soon Senate majority leader, vice president, and president.

A poor start in life does not block a person out. Several presidents were born in poverty: Jackson, Lincoln, Andrew Johnson, and James Garfield. Some others were born into struggling families: Truman, Eisenhower, Lyndon Johnson, and Bill Clinton among them.

Different explanations count for success; these are only a few.

Name _____ Date _____

Challenges

1. What three men lost presidential races at one time but won the job later?

_____

_____

2. Whose defeat in a senate race did not stop him from being elected president two years later?

_____

3. Of the five presidents listed, which ones were noted for charisma: John Adams, Andrew Jackson, William H. Taft, Theodore Roosevelt, Dwight Eisenhower?

_____

_____

4. What is meant by "availability"?

_____

_____

5. How might English classes help you become successful in politics?

_____

_____

_____

6. What person benefited and who was hurt by the economy in 1928 and 1932?

_____

_____

7. Who attracted notice as an assistant to a Congressman?

_____

8. Whose road to the White House began with an election as militia general?

_____

9. Which of these are good examples of men born in poverty: Andrew Jackson, Andrew Johnson, James Garfield, John Kennedy?

_____

_____

10. Which of these were born into struggling families: Thomas Jefferson, Harry Truman, Franklin Roosevelt, Bill Clinton?

_____

_____

Name _____ Date _____

Points to Consider

1. Do you think that "try, try, try again" works for everyone? If a person wants to try again, what should he or she do in between elections?

_____

_____

_____

_____

_____

2. What kinds of careers are opening up as ways for people to enter politics?

_____

_____

_____

_____

_____

3. Lyndon Johnson was given as an example of a person with persuasive skills. What other skills might help someone else to be elected to an office?

_____

_____

_____

_____

_____

Activity

Have the class think of examples of people who are *not* in politics who might have the charisma it takes to be a success. Sports stars and celebrities would be a good place to start.

Election Simulations

It is said: "Tell me something and I'll soon forget it. Show me something, and I'll likely forget it. Make me do something, and I'll never forget it." Teachers know this is true, and they try to create learning situations where students put into practice what they have learned.

Teaching politics to students too young to vote makes the desire to create simulations even stronger. Teachers have great imaginations and can devise a greater variety of situations than can be included here. The suggestions proposed are arranged from the simplest and least time-consuming to those that will take more time but may be more fun and broader learning experiences for students. The teacher may come up with variations that suit their situation better than these suggestions.

VARIATION 1 - FOLLOWING THE STATE CAMPAIGN TRAIL.

Take a campaign in your state for a U. S. Senate seat or a governor's race. On the map, mark where the candidates are campaigning and gather reports on what issues they discuss at each stop. Campaign headquarters for each candidate and party should be happy to supply information.

Your students might make up a list of questions they would ask the candidate if he or she came to your town; perhaps your interest will cause him or her to visit your class.

The students might hold a mock election for the school, with some presenting the case for each candidate. If the candidates know you are doing this and that it may appear in your local newspaper, they may send a representative to your school or come themselves.

The teacher should be careful to make sure that the supporters of each side are approximately equal in numbers and ability.

VARIATION 2 - FOLLOWING THE NATIONAL CAMPAIGN TRAIL.

Follow the current or most recent presidential campaign from beginning to end. Have the students gather information about each candidate running in the primary; some will soon drop out, and students should try to learn why. Go to the national convention (video tapes are made by each party of that event). Students see the convention process in action and get a "glossy view" of the candidates.

Many questions can be brought up. What kind of person makes the most successful candidate? Are the primary process and convention systems the best way to choose candidates? What issues are discussed, and what important issues are neglected? Why do some candidates fail and others succeed? To what extent has fund-raising been important in the process? Why was this particular vice-presidential candidate chosen?

VARIATION 3 - CREATING A CLASS CAMPAIGN.

Instead of following the campaigns of others, this approach will be more detailed and take more time, but it will be more exciting and involve students more. The basic concept is that students create their own candidate, give that candidate a background and positions on issues, and create their candidate's campaign.

CREATING THE CANDIDATE. Develop a family and career for the person. Give that person a face and personality that will win voter support. Students can give their candidate a family background, a home state, a college, a spouse and children, and a career that has brought him or her to national prominence and their party's nomination.

ISSUES. Make a list of issues that are sure to come up in a presidential campaign, then decide what stand the candidate should take on these issues. Students might talk to the biology teacher about environmental issues, to medical professionals on health issues, and to a businessman and a labor leader about business and foreign trade issues.

After deciding on a policy, they should make a list of who will support and who will oppose their position. Deciding that Group "X" will oppose them, is there any way they can create a position on some other issue that will make the candidate more acceptable to Group "X"? This will teach them to look at issues as politicians do.

CAMPAIGN. The campaign should be fun for students. They can work up campaign slogans, buttons, and literature. They can prepare speeches for their candidate. They will probably want to make commercials and prepare rallies for their choice.

Students could prepare an itinerary for their person and study the geography involved in a national campaign. The teacher can give them information that will cause problems for their campaign. For example, they have taken a pro-labor position. Their candidate is going to Los Angeles on a campaign swing. The teacher throws in a strike in Los Angeles where strikers have been charged with the murder of the factory owner. What will their candidate say in Los Angeles? They should also study the time factors involved in moving the candidate around and prepare an agenda for a day in the life of the candidate. Where the teacher sees a weakness, throw a monkey wrench into their plan.

Include the results of public opinion polls, business news, an international crisis, a scandal, perhaps a personal tragedy, and other variables that will keep the candidate's campaign team alert.

If two classes are working against each other, they might hold an assembly to present their candidates and try to persuade other students to back them. Students educating other students and exciting them about the political process will increase the enthusiasm for real candidates and real campaigns.

Answer Keys

The Anytown School Student Council Election (page 6)
1. To split the girls' vote so Bill can win
2. Fred realized he didn't have enough to win.
3. They knew it was a waste of effort to convince those who were loyal to the other side.
4. Laura is from Ritzy Hills, but Bill is a boy.
5. Bill is from the Valley and is poor like she is.
6. Victory over Bigandtall school's team
7. Laura promises to cut the school day by 15 minutes.
8. Activists made signs and tried to convince classmates.
9. If they raised hands, they would be less likely to vote the way they wanted.
10. Several possible answers that would be valid

Elections: The Basic Element of Democracy (page 10)
1. Government where the citizens make the decisions
2. It is too large for people to meet and decide.
3. The official may lose his job in the next election.
4. In tyranny, information is what the government tells them.
5. It required owning at least a certain amount of property before a person could vote.
6. To keep African-Americans and ignorant whites from voting
7. No one knows how he votes.
8. African-American men
9. Initiative
10. Recall

Comparing Election Systems (page 14)
1. 1864 and 1944
2. Commons, general election
3. Ruler (king or queen); chosen because they lead the largest party in Commons
4. Her Majesty's Loyal Opposition
5. It watches for mistakes by Cabinet.
6. U. S. president
7. Senate 6 years; House 2 years
8. Partisan has party labels, non-partisan does not
9. States
10. No

American Political Parties (page 18)
1. Washington
2. Madison
3. Special interests concerned with a short list of interests; political party with many
4. "B" recruited people to help his campaign.

5. Meet and work with others who are also interested in politics
6. National conventions
7. Choose presidential and vice-presidential candidates
8. National chairman
9. Democratic National Committee
10. Public relations, computerized mailing lists, research, and fund raising

The U. S. Two-Party System (page 22)
1. Federalists and Republicans
2. Jackson
3. Slavery
4. #2; It is practical.
5. #3; Loyalty of officeholders, or possibly #4; Rules favor them
6. #1; Tradition
7. Republicans 7, Democrats 6
8. The city
9. Republican
10. McGovern

Third Parties: The Political Wild Cards (page 26)
1. Nixon and Humphrey
2. Nixon
3. To get the election thrown into the House
4. Graduated income tax, direct election of senators, initiative, and recall
5. They supported the Democratic candidate.
6. Bull Moose
7. Perot, 19 percent
8. They don't think the third-party candidate can win.
9. Left-wing parties
10. One-issue party

Who Runs? (page 30)
1. Financial reward
2. Anger
3. See a need
4. Prestige
5. Power
6. Criticisms of public officials
7. Privacy
8. Views
9. Job
10. Time

Who Votes? (page 34)
1. Turnout will be higher in 2004; it's a presidential election year.
2. Stronger party loyalty

3. Seven million more voted; it was going to be a closer election.
4. Taxes; affect them personally (other acceptable answers might also be given)
5. Their children would be affected.
6. They would have to pay higher taxes.
7. Democrats
8. Great Plains and New England
9. The rich and middle class
10. To keep them from voting for "B"

State and Local Elections (page 38)
1. By party
2. Nonpartisan
3. Prosecutor; job more often mentioned in the press
4. Clerk
5. They have a particular service to provide.
6. The public didn't trust the legislature to make decisions that might limit their own powers.
7. Can save campaign funds for general election
8. Mayor
9. Businesses, unions, and special interests
10. Very little or none

Running for Congress (page 42)
1. Senator, 30; Representative, 25
2. 435; the House
3. Drawing district lines to benefit a party
4. Right to send mail free
5. The manager is in charge of staff and volunteers.
6. The pollster takes public opinion polls to discover attitudes on issues.
7. Finding out if there is enough support
8. A Senate candidate has to cover the whole state, and it has broader interests than a House district.
9. May demand a promise the candidate doesn't want to make
10. Being called "Senator"

Running for President (page 46)
1. 35 years old
2. J.Q. Adams, George W. Bush, Benjamin Harrison, and Franklin Roosevelt (any three)
3. Washington and Monroe
4. To clean up the mess in Washington
5. Blamed inflation and unemployment on too much government
6. Only registered party members
7. Allows registered voter to vote in any party's primary
8. 60 percent
9. They drop out.
10. Someone not seriously considered before

Organizing the Presidential Campaign (page 50)
1. Choosing a running mate who will bring wider support
2. Find someone better.
3. Yes; primary statements might cost votes among the general public.
4. Choosing the topics to be discussed
5. A stand popular in one place may cost votes somewhere else.
6. Lincoln-Douglas debates
7. Kennedy-Nixon in 1960
8. Don't want to make a mistake
9. Helped Harrison win
10. Two of the three: work cheap, do needed jobs, and bring enthusiasm

Financing the Campaign (page 54)
1. A bribe is money given to cause a person to do something immoral or wrong. Yes; it was given to them to vote in favor of their special interest.
2. People, not interests, should choose candidates.
3. Break-in at Democratic headquarters (Watergate)
4. $10 million primary, $20 million general [$30 million total]
5. Parties and PACs
6. Limited funds that can be given to candidates
7. Unlimited funds going to the candidate's party or PACs that support the candidate
8. $3 billion
9. $673,000
10. $4.7 million

The Media and Public Opinion Polls (page 58)
1. Reporters following the candidates
2. Find out who's ahead, and what issues are most important
3. More likely to get elected
4. Gives briefings, informal chats, and press handouts
5. Richard Nixon
6. Spiro Agnew
7. Associated Press
8. Candidate will say something witty or profound in hopes it will be used.
9. *Literary Digest*
10. The last poll was taken two weeks before the election.

The Electoral College (page 62)
1. 12 electors
2. State legislatures
3. The House chooses from the top three.
4. No. "E" won the election with electoral votes.
5. Small towns in big states, and to smaller states

6. "F" was probably going to lose Ohio.
7. Popularity is dropping there, so he wants to build it up.
8. To have pictures taken doing a farm chore
9. Posturing: assuming an attitude for effect
10. Yes

Expecting the Unexpected (page 66)
1. Bryan campaign in 1896 and Truman in 1948.
2. Everything a candidate has done is studied.
3. They were all older candidates who had to prove themselves.
4. He wants a landslide victory.
5. He does not want to be overwhelmingly defeated.
6. Fear of war
7. The support for Dr. King brought out the African-American vote.
8. It takes attention away from the campaign.
9. A blooper is stupid mistake.
10. Repeating same positions over and over

What Does It Take to Win? (page 70)
1. Jackson, Cleveland, and Nixon
2. Lincoln
3. Jackson, Roosevelt, Eisenhower
4. People most likely to be considered for high office
5. It will teach you to read, write, and speak better.
6. Hoover
7. Lyndon Johnson
8. Jackson
9. Jackson, Johnson, and Garfield
10. Truman and Clinton

Bibliography

A person wishing to do further reading on any topic has to start somewhere. One suggestion is to read about the subject in a good encyclopedia. At the end of the article, there will be suggestions for further reading. Go to one of those sources on the list, and you will discover at the back of the book the bibliography that the author has used. Footnotes at the bottom of the page or end of the chapter also give clues about where to find more information on that specific subject.

Many books have been written about elections and political parties in general and specific elections in particular. Most may be too difficult for some students to understand, but they might be used with help from the teacher. In addition to books about politics, magazines and newspapers will be on file for research on specific elections. In addition, the biographies of individual candidates often have detailed information that would be very useful to teacher and student.

Campaigns

Altschuler, Bruce. *Running in Place: A Campaign Journal.* Chicago: Nelson-Hall, 1996.

America Goes to the Polls: C-Span 1992 Election Calendar. Washington: C-Span, 1992.

Bean, Louis. *How to Predict Elections.* Westport, CN: Greenwood, 1972.

Bibby, John. *Politics, Parties and Elections in America.* Chicago: Nelson-Hall, 1996.

Black, Christine. *The Pursuit of the Presidency: 'Ninety-two and Beyond.* Phoenix: Oryx, 1993.

Boller, Paul. *Presidential Campaigns.* New York: Oxford, 1985.

Callaway, John (ed.). *Campaigning on Cue.* Chicago: University of Chicago, 1988.

Carroll, Susan. *Women as Candidates in American Politics.* Bloomington: Indiana University, 1994).

Christian, Spencer. *Electing Our Government.* New York: St. Martin, 1996.

Dunham, Patricia. *Electoral Behavior in the United States.* Englewood, N.J.: Prentice-Hall, 1990.

England, Robert. *So You Want to Run for Political Office ....* Greenfield Center, N.Y.: Greenfield Center, 1992.

Golden, Catherine. *The Campaign Manager: Running and Winning Local Elections.* Ashland, OR: Oak Street, 1996.

Goldman, Peter and Mathews, Tom. *Quest for the Presidency: The 1988 Campaign.* New York: Simon and Schuster, 1989.

Guide to U. S. Elections. Washington: Congressional Quarterly, 1994.

Karlberg, Britta. *Go Perot: The Diary of a Volunteer.* Monroe, N.Y.: Library Research, 1994.

Kelley, Stanley. *Interpreting Elections.* Princeton, N.J.: Princeton Univ., 1983.

Maisel, L. Sandy. *Parties and Elections in America: The Electoral Process.* New York: McGraw, 1993.

Nelson, Michael. *The Elections of Nineteen Ninety-Two* . Washington: Congressional Quarterly, 1993.

Orren, Gary. *Blurring the Lines: Candidates and Journalists in American Elections.* New York: Free Press, 1992.

Reichley, A. James. *Elections American Style.* Washington: Brookings, 1987.

Sullivan, George. *Choosing the Candidates.* Parsippany, N.J.: Silver Burdett, 1991.

Thurber, James and Nelson, Candice (eds.). *Campaigns and Elections American Style.* Boulder, CO: Westview, 1995.

Weisberg, Herbert. *Democracy's Feast: Elections in America.* Chatham, N.J.: Chatham House, 1995.

White, Theodore. *The Making of a President: 1960.* New York: Pocket Books, 1962. [First in a series of excellent books covering elections to 1992].

Political Parties

Beck, Paul and Sorauf, Frank. *Party Politics in America.* New York: Harper Collins, 1992.

Crotty, William (ed.). *Political Parties in Local Areas.* Knoxville: University of Tennessee, 1987.

Epstein, Leon. *Political Parties in the American Mold.* Madison: University of Wisconsin, 1986.

Guide to U. S. Elections. Washington: Congressional Quarterly, 1994.

Kruschke, Earl. *Encyclopedia of Third Parties in the United States.* Santa Barbara: ABC-CLIO, 1991.

Rosenstone, Steven. *Third Parties in America.* Princeton: Princeton University, 1984.